Story Building

A Practical Guide for Bringing the Power of Stories into Classrooms and Communities

By Drew Kahn

Bruce Fox, SUNY Buffalo State Photographer

First Edition *2018*
Second Edition *2019*
Third Edition *2020*

Print ISBN: 978-1-66784-577-7
eBook ISBN: 978-1-66784-578-4

All questions and comments regarding the contents of this book and requests for workshops, presentations and teacher training intensives must be in writing and directed to:

Anne Frank Project
SUNY Buffalo State
Campbell Student Union, Suite 400J
1300 Elmwood Avenue
Buffalo, NY 14222

Professor Drew Kahn can be contacted via email at: **kahnaj@buffalostate.edu**

AFP/Buffalo State students rehearse their story.

Confessions and Preparations

While I enjoy the writing process, at the end of the day I am a *Teacher*. I have been dragging my literary feet for several years before writing this book. I have been hesitant (to say the least) to share the story building process on paper. I feel most at home in the middle of the action. I would prefer to be teaching the work in the basement of a public school or musty studio in an old warehouse than writing about it from the comfy confines of my university office. I also have an unreasonable fear that if I were to write down what I have learned over the past three decades the work will stop being organic, necessary, or effective. Perhaps both 'reasons' were just me being lazy? Regardless, I have four ways of combatting my fears that you will note throughout the book:

1. I have had the most success communicating the work by teaching the work. I share the process through this book as a *Teacher*, so I write like I am teaching and you are on your feet learning. The multiple *#Breadcrumb Alerts#* are reflections of the classroom rhythm as they are ideas that must be attended to in the moment so proper context can be achieved. Each 'crumb' will not only support and inform the issue presently being taught, but it will also combine with other 'crumbs' to form the Anne Frank Project's (AFP) ethos and foundational philosophies…the 'loaf' if you will.

My hope is that the *#Breadcrumb Alerts#* will illuminate the present topic without derailing the lesson.

2. This book is a supplement to the practice of AFP's story building process. This is extremely important and will be impossible for me to manage so... *I'm trusting you.* You should only be reading this book AFTER you have personally, physically experienced the AFP story building process facilitated by an employee of the Anne Frank Project. This can happen in an AFP workshop, residency, semester-long course, or professional development training. This 'Do First, Think Second' sequence is at the heart of our philosophy. The nature of meaningful story building requires each participant to first experience the process kinesthetically followed by intellectual support; Heart first, head second. If you were to read this book first and then engage in the physical experience your brain will have convinced you that you 'know' the story building process and thus your physical commitment would be reduced, and your instrument would steer clear of anything new or risky. 'Knowing' is extremely overrated, and 'Doing' is extremely underrated. Do yourself a favor—if you are genuinely interested in this work and have not yet experienced it with your body, close this book and contact us at the Anne Frank Project. We will plug you into a story building experience and this book will be waiting for you after.

3. Returning to the world of food metaphors, I will be guiding you through preparation of the 'full meal' of a story; your plate will undoubtedly floweth over. This meal may involve steps, elements and time you don't have access to in your workplace. Story building is not an all or nothing process. Rather, it is a process that you can partake in at multiple

levels, from the simplest classroom moment to clarify an abstract topic to the creation of a full-length play; it is not an "all you can eat" meal, it is an "eat what you need" opportunity. Please, please, please never allow yourself to work under the cloud of educational guilt, "I'm a terrible teacher if I don't do every single thing I read in this book!"

Creating an entire play from start to finish might seem daunting—that's understandable. Story building is not like prescribing medication where the wrong dose can create serious problems. You will not hurt your students by delivering smaller doses of what you may have assumed the 'proper dose.' Building your "meal" one "helping" at a time may, in fact, be the best way to progress. Simple rule for this work: If you are using ANY element we share in this book that involves your students activating the class content with their bodies, you are invested in the process of story-building and story-based learning! Think of the "meal" of this book more like a "buffet," where you can eat whatever you like and whatever amount that is required to satisfy your appetite. As long as you are AT the buffet you are doing the right thing!! Bon appétit!

4. Most importantly, this book is a response to the demand from teachers and organizations that have experienced the positive impact of AFP's story-building process. We have bonded through common story and achieved great things together in compact times. Amidst the joys and tears that are typically expressed at the conclusion of our work together, a repeated question regularly surfaces: "What next?" If this question doesn't surface right away it will a few weeks after we have left. I get it. It is easier to apply the work of story-building when the AFP crew is present. The

schools and organizations have cleared the days, gathered participants, made flyers, and prepared their environments for us. Once the honeymoon is over, it's not so easy to apply the work. Our model provides possibilities for filling gaps in instruction, which means the work is outside the norm and difficult to maintain without reminders and support. There is nothing more liberating than our story-building communities (villages) collaborating, sharing, and creating together for a common purpose. Doing this alone or with fewer collaborators can be challenging. The demand for our work has, thankfully, grown beyond our ability to provide staffing for every request. This is especially true with the requests for follow-up workshops, trainings, and residencies. I am honored the Anne Frank Project's success has expanded our audience to hundreds of schools and colleges, several U.S states, international partnerships in Rwanda, Kenya and Switzerland and future international locations in Burma, India, and Viet Nam. So, the brilliant solution to this great problem: Write a book!

ANNE FRANK PROJECT

BUFFALO STATE · The State University of New York

Scan above to visit AFP Website

the **anne frank** project

Contents

*"How wonderful it is that nobody need wait
a single moment before starting to
improve the world."*

Anne Frank

Prologue I:
More Than 'Theater'

I am a Professor of Theater. There, I said it, admitted it, made it public. I feel better now. For the past 25 years it's always been a personal bone of contention. Not because I am ashamed of the title (quite the opposite!), but because the title has never said enough, never captured the true breadth of the gig I immerse myself in daily. The connotation of "Theater" has never sat well with me. The etymology is appropriately expansive: to behold, to view, to witness in the open air. Contemporary responses, however, conjure plush red velvet seats, expensive tickets, and phony British accents. Or perhaps the simple, justifiable idea of driving to the theater, sitting down in an arm-crossed grunt and awarding several review stars...thumbs up or down? "That sounds fun!" or "You get paid for that?" are typical responses. The fond pictures of a high school production of Grease or a recent trip to Broadway (or Disney, Las Vegas, etc.) burst through the mind accompanied by bright smiles. So what's the problem right? I mean who gets to announce their vocation and (almost) always get the positive Pavlovian pop!?! I'm not complaining. I love those things too. Rehearsing acting scenes, producing plays, wearing costumes and sword fighting under bright lights have all, thankfully, long been a part of my professional life. But that is and was never enough for me. Those traditional theater elements I repeated and refined for over three decades all prepared me for what I know now as the essence, responsibility, and heart of the work of this theater professor. Unbeknownst to me, this subconscious, lengthy rehearsal period was the incubator for refining the tools of drama in the theater so that I can now share the power of Story outside the theater.

I began my work as a professor in 1993 at SUNY (State University of New York) Buffalo State. Buffalo State is one of 64 campuses in the SUNY system and the only one located in an urban setting. With 12,000 primarily undergraduate students, the college attracts a diverse, raw, primarily first-generation college population. Our students come from all over New York State, dispersed between the New York City area and local, Western New York (Buffalo) folks. These kids come to us with a fire in their bellies. This was one of primary draws for me to leave sunny Los Angeles and come to Buffalo for my first professor gig. These weren't entitled teenagers expecting me to stay out of their way as they shuffled off to Broadway, oh no! These were kids from hard working, diverse families, representing multiple cultural, faith and socio-economic backgrounds. These were young people who were, usually, the first person in their families to go to college and knew they had to hold jobs during college to help make it a reality. There were no cheers when I announced I would be absent from a future class —they were wondering when I would be making that time up with them; after all they paid for it! I love my students at Buffalo State. I was planning on staying for a 'couple of years' and then moving on to share my 'brilliance' with other university campuses. Those 'couple of years' evolved into 25 years and counting. Buffalo is where I met my best-friend-soul-sharing-wife, where we raised our beautiful children and where we are embraced by a city authentically committed to *community*.

Yes, a community under a coating of cold white stuff longer than we would like each year; a small price to pay for the warmth we receive. I can certainly extend my 'I Love Buffalo' story, but for the purpose of the book, professionally speaking, let's focus on Buffalo State, which has always shared a common passion for the power of story and its multiple applications. Our campus has undergone numerous administrative changes and shifts in academic philosophies; Buffalo State is not immune to the game of higher-ed popcorn played nationally. Thankfully, I have experienced a common thread of support for my research. This was not blind charity. Alongside a wide array of gifted academics, teachers and artists, our theater program has grown significantly in size, impact and reputation since 1993. Professional quality theater productions are valuable currency on a university campus; the importance of public art's potential to create unique opportunities for marketing, fundraising and community relations cannot be overstated. Again, the subconscious building towards what I now do was at play here. I was never trying to bank for my future research in story—I was only acting on the nagging gut reminder that 'Theater' was not enough. As chair of the department during our important growth periods my overarching objective was to provide a demanding environment where our faculty could lead our students through the creation of high-quality theater. Period. This objective was supported (sometimes easier than others-the Arts must advocate in academia!) because we provided results; we created an excellent curricular training sequence, produced exciting productions, and our students worked professionally. Buffalo State recognized this low-hanging fruit, but also always supported the 'something more' idea, that Story *really* improves lives and that this fruit growing on higher branches may one day be within our reach. I have accepted interviews for positions elsewhere—each time I am reminded of my good fortune at Buffalo State. After all, I would hardly call my research traditional—it requires risk and trust. I think of my campus as more than an employer—they have always been and continue be my partner in story. This partnership is illustrated best by the creation of the Anne Frank Project.

Academic theater departments must always be a season ahead for planning purposes. Buffalo State's department is not unique in that aspect. What is unique about our program is that we include the students in the show selection process. This is in keeping with the philosophy of the importance of community. Theater is a communal process and for a liberal arts theater department to deny any community-building teaching opportunity always seemed criminal to me, or at the very least, educationally negligent. Most academic theater programs conduct what I call "Mountain Top" decision-making. You know, we the almighty professor gods deem what's necessary for our plebeian students from the mountaintop of hubris and throw our thunderbolts of conviction at the students because we know what's best! I understand why most programs operate like this: It's easier! You will note throughout this book that I have learned to mistrust ease. Doing good work is hard work—I am suspicious when it is not. Now please don't misunderstand, this is not a free for all, recreation of Woodstock like process…no, no, no. My students will phrase it another way, rolling their eyes as they share a favorite quote of mine, "There can be no freedom without discipline."

> ### #Breadcrumb Alert#
>
> *I will be sharing multiple quotations with you that have fueled my teaching process over the years. They are shared with you for two reasons: 1) They may provide inspiration for you and your students. 2) They are excellent examples of how large ideas can be condensed into short phrases; this is a key concept for all of story-building that I will return to later.*

Returning to the play selection process: there are indeed rules, students do have input, the faculty operate from a 'what's best for the students' perspective and rely on their knowledge and experience of drama to steer the process. In the fall of 2005, the faculty and students of Buffalo State's theater department gathered to discuss next year's season of plays. We were presently in the midst of a season of plays that included a contemporary comedy, an 18th century mannered love scandal and an outlandish rock musical. All these plays had fun styles for the students to learn, but did not demand intense, in-depth emotional journeys. For that reason, I proposed we produce *The Diary of Anne Frank*. After an understandable discussion of production concepts, casting concerns and performance demands it was agreed—we would include *The Diary of Anne Frank* in our 2006-7 season at Buffalo State Theater.

> ### #Breadcrumb Alert#
>
> *Because you are a story-building animal, you are putting the pieces together, creating a story and you're correct: This production was the genesis for what is now the Anne Frank Project. You couldn't stop putting the pieces together even if you tried because your brain is wired for story.*

What I am sure you don't yet know is *how* this play became the project. I am sure of this because I didn't know it either. I half-jokingly refer to the Anne Frank Project as the greatest professional mistake of my life. *Half*-jokingly because I believe fate, destiny, and all of that other spiritual stuff we claim to understand but don't is serious and at work. I have surrendered to the fact that it cannot be predicted or consciously manipulated no matter how much I try—that's kind of the whole point. Our desire to control, organize and know how these things work is an excellent example of how we use and depend on story.

> *#Breadcrumb Alert#*
>
> *We tell stories for many important reasons. At the primal level, we use stories to bring order to chaos, to create certainty where there is fear and provide answers to mysteries. I could really stop right there because those are THE primary reasons we create and share stories. I imagine, by now, you know I won't stop there.*

The idea of directing *The Diary of Anne Frank* terrified and excited me. It terrified me because I was raised in a traditional Jewish American home where the Holocaust was a crucial piece of our tribe's identity, history and spirit. The attempted (and nearly successful) complete extermination of our people was placed on the highest shelf of sanctity. The personal stakes could not have been higher. I was excited to bring the numerous life lessons from the heart of this amazing young girl to a diverse audience. I was excited to break the image of Anne Frank as a 'celebrity' of the Holocaust by re-introducing the audience to the girl, the person. I was excited to immerse my students in the intense demands of owning the emotional realities of these characters. I was excited to tell the human stories of these real people beyond the mandate of a 7th grade reading list. Because the terror/excitement factor wasn't high enough (yeah right) I had a strong conviction that, in order to deliver the most relevant production, we needed to provide a context for the story that would not allow the audience to rest in the 'knowing.' The predictability of well-known stories often releases the audience from any surprises, any discoveries and most importantly, any personal responsibility. From my standpoint, this was unacceptable. I have never been a fan of what I call 'museum theater,' which involves staging popular plays with overused, expected production values. These productions seem be snapshots directly out of Theater 101 texts; no surprises, exactly as the audience might have imagined (*zzzzzz*). This is a missed opportunity. Those duplicated sets, costumes and lights were unique and completely original *once*. When initially created they were birthed and imagined from an inspiration, a production-driven *reason* that was meant to propel the story forward. This is how style happens in art—it is organically created to help tell the story most beautifully. When story ideas are repeated simply to repeat them as a convenience, the event distances itself from its true purpose: to engage the audience in a meaningful lesson they can witness in theatrical beauty so that they can apply it to their world, their communities and their lives.

> #### #Breadcrumb Alert#
>
> *Building impactful, meaningful stories is hard work. When choices are made out of convenience and what might be easier, the story's impact and value will be forever diminished. Concessions are what are sold in the lobby of the theater, not what is made during the creation of impactful stories.*

So, the challenges with our production (since the director refused to descend from his anti-repetition soapbox) were:

1. How to tell Anne Frank-the-girl story vs. Anne Frank-the-celebrity story.

2. How to tell the story in a fresh, exciting way that would engage responsibility.

3. How to tell the story to a diverse, colorful audience of 18–22-year-old college students.

Regarding the final challenge: American academic theater departments spend an inordinate amount of time and energy producing plays written by white men about white men for white men. It is no wonder our non-white college students often feel disengaged during these productions. I would too if I couldn't find 'me' on stage. College theatre is as guilty of white-as-neutral as America itself. If you believe that the theater is a microcosm of society, then there you have it—pretty clear, right? I don't bring this up as a political commentary, I bring it up as obvious fact. This is a problem in general of course, but a particularly dangerous problem on a campus as diverse as SUNY Buffalo State. Indeed, if we are to 'celebrate our differences (mission)' we must activate this principle in the theater. We must provide stories where *all* our students can see themselves on stage.

So, with an amazing play based on an amazing story and a set of challenges to shape our production, I dove into research. What was the *world* of the production where all these boxes could be checked? What was going to be the context of the production? What was going to be our production *concept*? *Concept* is a word thrown around liberally amongst us artist types. Here's my definition: *The controlling idea that shapes how each element of the story is shared with the audience.* Placing *Romeo and Juliet* in the middle of the Israeli/Palestinian conflict would be a *concept*. Having a jazz band playing live on stage as part of *A Streetcar Named Desire* would be concept. Dressing the cast from the musical *Oklahoma!* in futuristic alien costumes would be concept. The director's job is to bring the ideas to the production team so the designers (set, costume, lights, sound) all have a clear understanding of the world of our production...the concept.

Great stories, great novels and great plays are about the same thing: Problems... lots and lots of problems. If the story unfolds without problems, conflicts, and complications the audience will lose interest. We love the obstacles our heroes must overcome to achieve their objectives. No conflict, no drama. We have an insatiable appetite for tragedy and tension. The higher the stakes, the worse-off it is for the characters, the better it is for the story. There can be no greater conflict than genocide.

#Breadcrumb Alert#

Genocide in particular and oppression in general are powerful fuel for the work of story-building. When we discuss genocide in the schools the students immediately respond personally. Not because they have personal connections to the historical atrocities, but because they have personal connections to the ingredients that cause genocide. Their oppressions are surfaced through the stories of others. I have never worked with a student who lacked oppression.

"There is no(thing) better than adversity. Every defeat, every heartbreak, every loss, contains its own seed, its own lesson on how to improve your performance the next time. "

—Malcolm X

I immersed myself in the unforgiving and haunting world of genocide. The results clarified and shook me to the core. While each genocide of the 20th century was unique, they all shared some clear commonalities. These universal ingredients immediately sparked questions in my mind: "How many diaries of innocent children who perished during genocides do we *not* have?" "How many 'Anne Franks' have we missed?" "Is there an 'Anne Frank' in every genocide?"

Consider these common elements of genocide:

- What groups are always present?
- Perpetrators
- Victims
- Heroes
- Bystanders (largest group in every conflict)

What ingredients must be present? All 'successful' genocides must be:

- Planned
- Organized
- Supported
- **Good People Doing Nothing** (this is the most crucial)

As I combed through books, articles, documentaries and interviews I became an unwilling 'expert' in 20th century atrocities: The Turkish Genocide, Stalin's Forced Famine, Hitler's Holocaust, Pol Pot's Cambodia, Bosnia Herzegovina and Rwanda. Each devastating in its cruel attempts to erase 'the other.' Each mind boggling in the millions and millions of precious lives lost. Each eerily abiding by the common elements listed above—so simple, so tragic, and so obvious. Could we weave these universal truths into the fabric of our production without disrespecting Anne Frank? It was 2006, 12 years after the 1994 Genocide Against the Tutsi in Rwanda, yet we in the U.S. knew so little about this horrific current event. The students who were going to watch and perform in the play were alive yet knew little beyond the movie *Hotel Rwanda* as a reference point (we have since come to learn that much of this movie was based on several inaccuracies). Not only did this genocide happen in their lifetime, but it involved Africans; people who looked like many of our students so they could see themselves in the story. After much internal debating, our concept was chosen: We would have two 'Anne Franks' in our production: The Jewish girl hiding from the Nazis in World War II that we are familiar with and a Tutsi girl hiding from Hutu extremists during the 1994 Genocide Against the Tutsi in Rwanda. While I could share more details of this conceptual journey with you, for the purpose of this book, the above choice for including Rwanda in our 2006 production of *The Diary of Anne Frank* will stop here.

This was a choice, however, that has fueled our story well beyond this production. Rwanda's story of reconciliation is nothing short of remarkable. As I write this book 25 short years after the genocide, Rwanda is a model for the rest of the world to learn from. Every measurable aspect of their country has not only recovered but is in fact thriving. Rwanda is the fastest growing economy and the safest country in Africa. In 1994 there were three universities in Rwanda, there are now over 40. There are more women in political power in Rwanda than any country in the world! Is everything perfect in this tiny East African country the size of Vermont? Absolutely not. You will find no shortage of naysayers who believe Rwanda's success is the result of a nefarious political regime. These reports are often written by academics in their offices having never stepped foot on Rwanda soil. Having visited

Rwanda twice a year for the past decade, I can only share with you what I know and feel. Rwanda's people and resurgence is authentic and beautiful. I could go on and on, but it is important to leave you with what I see as the three building blocks for all of their success: *Reconciliation, Forgiveness and Community*. Imagine a country built on those principles! Imagine the poignant reflective possibilities with the Holocaust. Imagine seeing both 'Anne Franks' on stage reciting the words from Anne's diary side-by-side. Imagine Anne's words "I feel the suffering of millions. And yet, when I look up at the sky, I somehow feel that everything will change for the better, that this cruelty too shall end, that peace and tranquility will return once more." Perhaps Anne Frank was imagining such a place as Rwanda.

Rwanda Landscape
Rwanda is called the 'Land of a Thousand Hills.'

Hand Circle ISHYO, Kigali, Rwanda
Buffalo State students story-building with Rwandan Students

Production 'Annes' Side-by-Side

This production still holds the attendance record for Buffalo State's theater department. The student, faculty, staff and community response was overwhelming. While it was my responsibility as the director to create and sell the concept, it was our production team of designers and technicians and an inspired student cast of actors that deserve the credit—they embraced the work with an uncanny sense of personal ownership and devoted spirit. Perhaps the most inspired audience members were from our campus senior administration. Our President, Provost and Chief Diversity Officer were clear about the impact of this production, illustrated by emails like: 'This play is Buffalo State, this production activates our mission!" Every college campus in America has its mission—very few have physical evidence of that mission to share with others so readily. I was asked if we could re-stage this production each year. This was a great compliment, but not feasible. What nerves did we hit, however, that could be repeated? The universality of the human condition, the searching for solutions to conflict, the need for goodness to unite and the authentic hope for a peaceful future all seemed worth repeating. What vehicle could we create to showcase Anne Frank's own words "How wonderful it is that we need not wait a single moment before starting to change the world?" As I mentioned to the President in a meeting following the production with far too much bravado, "Aren't Anne Frank's words the whole point of what we are doing at Buffalo State?!?" That conversation could have gone several ways, not all of them vocationally positive. As you already know I am still employed by Buffalo State—whew! The President challenged me to create something new. Following several meetings discussing possibilities, several conferences testing possibilities and several grant applications to pay for the possibilities we had a result: In 2009 our first reincarnation of that 2006 production of *The Diary of Anne Frank*, a conference rallying around the theme "How wonderful it is that we need not wait a single moment before starting to change the world," a conference called, *The Anne Frank Project*.

Fast forward ten years and ten conferences to 2018: We now call our annual diversity conference our 'social justice festival' where we have welcomed artists, activists, authors, educators, business leaders and speakers from all over the world to share their stories with over 40,000 attendees from our campus and surrounding communities. Our format mandate that each session include interactive applications has created our reputation as the 'un-conference;' we like that. We never want attendees to sit, listen, take notes and apply the lessons someday. We insist that our audiences leave the festival each year having already been part of the process to 'improve the world.' This brain to body focus is central to all our work in the *Anne Frank Project*. It's really not a stroke of kinesthetic brilliance—it is the nature of what we do as story-builders in the theater. This story-centricity is also a key component of the festival; we believe every discipline has a story to share and are intrigued by the multiple ways in which we tell these stories. This is not a theater festival. This is a social justice festival where story is emphasized to assist in activating theory into action.

Good stories beget more stories. "So, what's next?" became a popular refrain after each year's festival. This was the opportunity to scratch that "something more than theater" nagging itch. The festival was its own story each year—of course it was, that's really all I know how to do. It wasn't like I was trying to create a brilliant business plan—it was using story as the structure for everything....*everything*. As the festival's evolution unfolded and the college continued its support, our little play expanded into a multi-layered, social justice initiative with programming throughout the year including:

Annual student trip to Rwanda, Africa

We had talked about it enough throughout and after the production—it was time to go! My initial trip in 2009 changed my life. I went with Carl Wilkens, the only American that stayed in Rwanda during the genocide. Carl saved the lives of many orphans those 100 days in 1994. I always tell people "going to Rwanda with Carl Wilkens is like going to a rock concert with Mick Jagger—-you get into places most others don't." Carl has since become a dear friend and part of the AFP family. We have travelled to Rwanda several times together and he has presented several times at our social justice festival. As I write this we have taken over 75 students to Rwanda to immerse ourselves in their amazing recovery process, experience the truth about East Africa and train Rwandan teachers to use Story-Based Learning in their classrooms. To date we have trained over 300 Rwandan teachers and reached over 30,000 students with the story-building work. I am sure we learn more from them than they do from us. We are thankful for the unwavering support and friendship from the Rwanda Ministry of Education and Office of the Mayor in Muhanga.

Play Building Curricular Sequence at Buffalo State

Upon returning from Rwanda, the students spend the following semester in a course with me entitled *Ensemble Theater* at Buffalo State. The purpose is threefold:

- To process their intense Rwanda experiences together as a community for a full semester.

- To share their Rwanda story with the campus community with individual presentations. They must condense their enormous, profound experiences into a single theme or lesson.

To create a story together inspired and informed by their trip to Rwanda to be performed at area high schools. These are not necessarily plays about Rwanda, but rather, performances sharing the powerful lessons learned in Rwanda (i.e. *How compassion leads to forgiveness* or *The power of community*).

Play and Workshop Tours

The play that was created in the Ensemble Theater class will tour local high schools. A new section of Ensemble Theater provides the vehicle where students also create an interactive workshop to follow the play's performance. This workshop engages the high school students in the physical practicing of the lessons in the play. For instance, a workshop teaching physical communication using body statues following a performance about self-image, peer pressure and conformity.

Story-Based Learning

THIS is the focus of this book and what I am eager to share with you! Based on the play building model we use to create our touring plays; we train teachers how to bring story into their classrooms as a curricular vehicle. This method moves the lesson content from the student's brains to the to their hearts by using their bodies to enable authentic, complete learning. This training is used across the disciplines and in multiple teaching environments. This is currently the busiest aspect of AFP where we have trained teachers and community leaders throughout the United States as well as Rwanda, Kenya, South Africa, Burma, Turkey, and Switzerland. AFP is in-residence in several schools in Buffalo, New York and is currently creating permanent training centers in Rwanda, Kenya, Switzerland, and the University of Missouri. Future possible training destinations include Burma, Viet Nam, and India.

Not bad for a university play, right? I am deeply proud of the organic creation and growth of the Anne Frank Project. It is more about the AFP family than any one individual. There are many lessons at play here. The most important are:

- Stories Matter

- WE before ME

- Listen to Your Students

- *Education without the body is memorization, not learning*

AFP's Mission:

The Anne Frank Project uses stories as vehicles for community building, conflict resolution, and identity exploration. Inspired by the wisdom of Anne Frank, AFP surfaces, creates and shares stories stifled by oppression.

AFP's Vision:

SUNY Buffalo State's Anne Frank Project will be an internationally recognized leader in progressive, experiential education and innovative professional development known for:

- It's highly effective, story-driven approach to learning in the K-12 and higher education arenas.

- It's highly effective, story-driven approach to organizational management in the professional, community and public arenas.

- Developing caring, inclusive, and nurturing communities, inspired by Anne Frank and dedicated to making her dream of an "improved world" a reality.

AFP's Values:

We, the Anne Frank Project family, community, and village are committed to:

- Providing story-based resources to marginalized individuals, organizations and communities;

- Excellent learning experiences in and out of the classroom;

- Kinesthetically moving theory to action;

- Being student and individual centered;

- Sharing the stories and cultures of non-western nations, people and communities;

- Respecting diversity and individual differences;

- Active social responsibility;

- Realizing our world's shared humanity;

- Teaching the discipline necessary to make positive change in the world;

- Representing Buffalo State and the SUNY system with respect, grace and honor.

Tell me and I forget.
Teach me and I remember.
***Involve** me and I learn.*

-Chinese Proverb

I am excited to share the tools and vocabulary of AFP's proven and award-winning story-building techniques. As you move through the following pages, please know my sincere hope is that you use this method to **involve** yourself, your students and community members in the beautiful and rewarding process of building stories!

Buffalo State/AFP Students dancing during their story
When the Walls Come Down—TRUTH!

*"The proper words in the proper places
are the true definition of style."*

Jonathan Swift

Prologue II:
Definitions and Terminology

When I was young boy growing up in Los Angeles, I remember my first trip to Dodger stadium. I wasn't then nor did I ever become a big baseball fan, but I remember, with crystal clarity, the ambience of the ballpark. As we walked down the cement steps to find our seats, the majesty of the event was in full swing (pun intended): the huge green field covered in a light hazy mist, the giant players warming up in their crisp uniforms, the busy pregame rituals of the stadium staff and the terrific sounds of the barking food and souvenir sellers. The one I remember most was "Programs, get your programs! Can't follow the game without a program!" So, we purchased a single program that proved to be our trusted guide throughout our nine-inning journey that day. Whenever we were lost, we knew where to go for the who's-who and what's-what. Here in *Prologue II* I hope to provide you with the same trusted resource.

Since us humans have been sharing oral stories for over 100,000 years, it's safe to say we are on to something here. What makes this number even more astounding is that we have been crafting these stories in basically the same way for the same duration. Kurt Vonnegut famously theorized there are only three plots in the world from which all stories are based. In 1959 Foster-Harris asserted that there are indeed only three basic plot patterns, and later Christopher Booker confidently claimed after 34 years of research that all literature stems from *The Seven Basic Plots* in his 2004 book of the same name. In a more recent study, the University of Vermont's Computational Story Lab found that there are in fact "six core trajectories which form the building blocks of all complex narratives." This is a debate that has been going on for hundreds of years and will, undoubtedly continue for many more…a story unto itself! My point here is the *What* stories are is magically simple. The *How* and *Why* we create and share stories is infinitely more complex; Yes, even more complex than nine innings of professional baseball.

The narrative world is filled with a wide variety of terminology and instructive models. After all, why does every English teacher use a different definition for 'theme?' My attempt here is to share, explain and unpack the language and approaches that have best served our work in building stories through the years.

#Breadcrumb Alert#

You will note that an essential ingredient to every step of the story-building process is **collaboration**. *The community voice fuels every moment.*

You will also note that teaching is just talking unless teachers model what they are requesting of their students. We must walk the walk or it will be perceived as inauthentic.

This is not 'my' story-building model. It is the collection of multiple philosophies, perspectives, experiences, and collaborations. The research foundation I share with you in this chapter lists several of my 'go to' resources as we move through the work. The creators of these models are some of my heroes. There is not enough paper to share the thousands of students, teachers, artists, colleagues, community members and friends who have contributed to the AFP story-building model. I will use the terms 'us' and 'we' as often as possible to remind you of the collaborative muscle behind the work. I will only be sharing the stuff that has worked and omitting my many mistakes—you're welcome.

Augusto Boal: Theatre of the Oppressed

"The purpose of Theatre of the Oppressed is to rehumanize humanity."— *Augusto Boal*

Created by Brazilian theatre visionary and Nobel Peace Prize nominee Augusto Boal (1931-2009), *Theatre of the Oppressed* is a form of popular community-based education that uses theater as a tool for social change. Originally developed out of Boal's revolutionary work with peasant and worker populations in Latin America, it is now used all over the world for social and political activism, conflict resolution, community building, therapy, and government legislation. It is also practiced on a grassroots level by community organizers, activists, teachers, social workers, cultural administrators and more.

Inspired by the vision of Paulo Freire and his 1968 landmark treatise on education *Pedagogy of the Oppressed, Theatre of the Oppressed* invites critical thinking. It is about analyzing rather than accepting, questioning rather than giving answers. It is also about taking action — "acting" rather than just talking. The audience is not made of passive spectators but instead active "spect-actors" invited on stage to explore and activate potential solutions for the issues at hand.

Boal's books have been translated into over 35 languages and the work radiates from his original *Center for Theatre of the*

Oppressed in Rio de Janeiro as well as centers in the United States, Canada, England, India, Germany, Austria, Sweden, Holland, Italy, Afghanistan, Turkey, Burkina Faso, and many others.

Two specific *Theater of the Oppressed* techniques regularly used and adapted for the work of AFP are:

Image Theatre

A series of physical exercises and games designed to uncover essential truths, opinions, and observations about society, culture and self. Using their own and others' bodies as "clay," participants create "human sculptures" — frozen images representing their experiences, feelings, ideas, oppressions, and/or dreams for the future.

Forum Theatre

A conflict-management technique where an unresolved scene of oppression is presented first, then replayed with the audience invited to stop the action, replace the character they feel is oppressed, struggling, or lacking power, and improvise alternative solutions. This structure, probably the most famous in *Theatre of the Oppressed* library, can be used to explore past and current situations or as a rehearsal tool to develop the story being worked on.

The work of Augusto Boal is a vital reference and inspiration for the story-building work of AFP. When describing our work to new audiences I often try to break it down to its simplest form, saying "We use the power of stories and theater *outside* of the theater to assist groups in overcoming their struggles." This explanation is derived from the 'Grandfather' of social justice theater, Augusto Boal and the 'Peace-Corp' of story, *Theatre of the Oppressed*.

Joseph Campbell: Power of the Myth

"We must let go of the life we have planned, so as to accept the one that is waiting for us." —Joseph Campbell

Joseph Campbell was an American mythologist, writer and lecturer best known for his work in comparative mythology and religion. His work covers many aspects of the human experience. His philosophy is often summarized by his phrase: "Follow your bliss," an idea, he asserts, that all heroes in every myth are bound to, whether they are conscious of it or not.

For Joseph Campbell, the study of myth was the exploration of the possibilities of consciousness. His lifetime of scholarship was nothing less than the search for the Holy Grail of radiant living. The dialog between Joseph Campbell and Bill Moyers that became *The Power of the Myth* was an event that changed many lives—mine included. It is more than a presentation of fascinating stories from all over the world. It is a vision of a rich inner life available to anyone willing to go on the initiatory adventures.

Perhaps Campbell's greatest influence on the work of AFP is the psychological significance of myth (story) on all of us. He asserted that myths show us how to live a human lifetime under any circumstances. It is this pedagogical function of mythology that carries the individual through the various stages and crises of life, from childhood dependency to the responsibilities of maturity, to the reflection of old age, and finally, to death. It helps people grasp the unfolding of life with integrity and grace. It initiates individuals into the order of realities in their own psyches, guiding them toward enrichment and realization.

In *The Power of the Myth* Joseph Campbell explores with Bill Moyers what enduring myths can tell us about our lives. In each of six episodes –"The Hero's Adventure," "The Message of the Myth," "The First Storytellers," "Sacrifice and Bliss," "Love and the Goddess," and "Masks of Eternity" — Moyers and Campbell focus on a character or theme found in cultural and religious mythologies. Campbell argues that these timeless archetypes continue to have a powerful influence on the choices we make and the ways we live.

In all of Campbell's work he consistently circles back to the 'hero's journey' we are all experiencing everyday of our lives (Something Campbell focuses on entirely and beautifully in his must read *The Hero With A Thousand Faces*). We join hands with Oedipus, Hamlet, Luke Skywalker, Snow White, Shrek, Bilbo Baggins, Mary Poppins, and Harry Potter on this archetypical, undeniable quest every day. This, Campbell would argue, and I would enthusiastically agree, is not presented for our entertainment, but rather, as a universal recipe for navigating the complexities of our lives. The hero's journey (below) is the first thing I share with my students on the first day of class. They can immediately plug themselves and their current journey (college) into the structure. They often wish they had seen this structure earlier in their lives, as "it would have made things so much easier!"

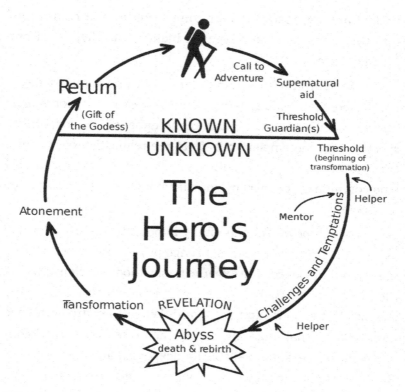

*Note:

I will dive more deeply into the intricacies and use of the Hero's Journey as well as other story structures during the during **Chapter/ Act II: Creating the Story.**

Contemplative Education

> *"The senses are of the earth, the reason stands apart from them in contemplation."*—*Leonardo da Vinci*

Contemplative pedagogy empowers students to integrate their own experience into the theoretical material they are being taught in order to cultivate and develop attention, deepen their understanding, foster greater connection to and compassion for others, and engender engaged inquiry into their most profound questions.

This is an education that promotes the exploration of meaning, purpose and values and seeks to serve our common human future. An education that enables and enhances personal introspection and contemplation leads to the realization of our inextricable connection to each other, opening the heart and mind to true community, deeper insight, sustainable living, and a more just society.

Though powerful and vitally important, the conventional methods of scientific research, pedagogy, and critical scholarship need to be broadened. The experiential methods developed within the contemplative traditions offer a rich set of tools for exploring the mind, the heart, and the world. When they are combined with conventional practices, an enriched research methodology and pedagogy become available for deepening and enlarging perspectives, leading to lasting solutions to the problems we confront. None of these methods require an ideology or creed and each is available equally to all.

Contemplative Practices in Higher Education by Daniel Barbezat and Mirabai Bush is essential reading for anyone interested in addressing contemporary education dilemmas and outdated teaching models. It is not breaking news that we are teaching today's young people with yesterday's tools and structures. If we are truly interested in preparing students for the multiple challenges of their lives, then we must broaden our definition of 'learner' to include the heart, soul, and body in addition to the mind. The whole student is addressed in contemplative education in an environment where their thoughts, ideas, and stories matter. Contemplation, introspection, and kinesthetic experience are hallmarks of contemplative education and essential characteristics of quality story-builders and their creative process.

The Tree of Contemplative Practices (below) offers a lovely metaphor for the process and journey of contemplative education.

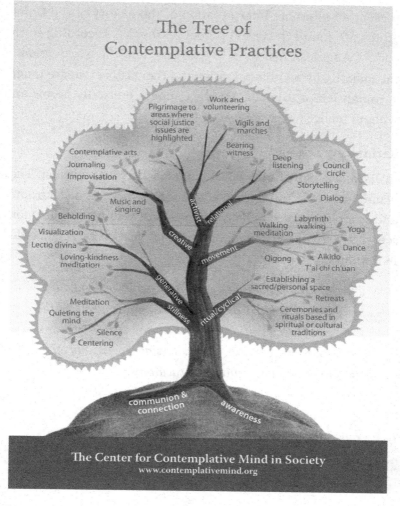

Three other resources that deserve mention beyond the bibliography due to the frequency they are used to feed the work of AFP are:

People's History of the United States by Howard Zinn

"The cry of the poor is not always just, but if you don't listen to it, you will never know what justice is." —Howard Zinn

American historian and political scientist Howard Zinn seeks to present an alternate interpretation of the history of the United States not found in typical school textbooks. According to the author, American history is to a large extent the exploitation of the majority by an elite minority and the 'history' we are taught is romanticized to make America appear eternally heroic and without malice.

Rethinking Schools

In 1986, a group of Milwaukee-area teachers had a vision. They wanted not only to improve education in their own classrooms and schools, but also to help shape reform throughout the public school system in the United States. Today that vision is embodied in Rethinking Schools.

> *"Rethinking Schools is a nonprofit publisher and advocacy organization dedicated to sustaining and strengthening public education through social justice teaching and education activism. Our magazine, books, and other resources promote equity and racial justice in the classroom. We encourage grassroots efforts in our schools and communities to enhance the learning and well-being of our children, and to build broad democratic movements for social and environmental justice."*
>
> —Rethinking Schools Mission.

They have an excellent website filled with resources. I subscribe to their monthly magazine that always sparks inspiration. This is an awesome resource for educators or anyone who cares about education reform in the U.S.

Coincidentally (or not), Rethinking Schools also publishes *A People's History for the Classroom*, based on the work of Howard Zinn this program helps teachers introduce students to a more accurate, complex, and engaging understanding of U.S. history than is found in traditional textbooks and curricula. One happy club, right?

#Breadcrumb Alert#

All kidding aside, this overlapping of ideas is far more than a 'club' of hippie liberals. As you enter the world of social justice education you will undoubtedly bump into repeated motifs, experts and resources. This is an inescapable truth for two reasons: 1) Great work has earned its reputation for a reason—its worthwhile and will contribute to your projects in time-tested ways. 2) Great stories beget more great stories. This is another universal law of story. I always tell my students that the best review they can receive from an audience member is "Me too." Once our personal library has been alerted by similar experiences we cannot wait to share our version of that experience...our story. It's why we interrupt a story presented in informal arenas (parties, bars, meals) before they are completed— 'Me too' needs to share!

Teaching Tolerance

Teaching Tolerance is a project of the Southern Poverty Law Center where educators who care about diversity, equity and justice can find news, suggestions, conversation and support. This is another jam-packed website with terrific resources, publications, film kits and professional development opportunities. Like Rethinking

Schools, they publish a very worthwhile monthly magazine that I admire. They advocate with passion and provide multiple network opportunities for like-minded educators, professional and caring citizens. I am especially fond of their literacy-based curriculum *Perspectives for a Diverse America* that provides detailed resources for building learning plans, connecting the standards to an anti-bias framework and accessing a diverse central text anthology. I find *Teaching Tolerance* to be particularly adept at responding to current injustice issues as they happen so that teachers have resources and vocabulary to begin those difficult conversations like LGBT rights, Islamophobia, refugee myths, police on Black violence and transgender bathroom legislation. Context and language may be Teaching Tolerance's greatest strengths.

I love just about everything Teaching Tolerance offers *except* their name. 'Tolerance" is a dated term in the world of human rights and social justice. I presume they have kept this word in their title because of their roots in the Southern Poverty Law Center. Founded in 1971 "to ensure that the promise of the civil rights movement became a reality for all." The idea of tolerance in 1971 was brave and appropriate for the time. Since their inception the SPLC has won landmark victories for the civil rights movement in the U.S. Headquartered in America's birthplace of civil rights, Montgomery Alabama, SPLC remains a beacon of humanity and advocacy for all who experience hate and bias.

That said, I still have a problem with the word "tolerance." We can do better than tolerate each other, can't we? If tolerance is the ultimate goal, then there is an assumption that the prejudice each side comes to the conflict with is justified. Yeah, I know you hate each other and that's not going to change, but could you at least *tolerate* each other? Does 'tolerance' as the end goal seem to validate the initial bias? I may be making too much of this one word, but I'm a story guy and words are important. What we name our organizations is the title of the story we want to tell. We named ours the 'Anne Frank Project' after all. I always tell my students, never complain without offering solutions—*meet complaints with collaborations.* So Southern Poverty Law Center, I offer you alternative titles for your excellent organization *Teaching Tolerance* that represent a more substantial end goal for the work you do:

Teaching Love

Teaching Unity

Teach Shared Humanity

Teaching Community

Teaching Love

(I realize I repeated the first one, it's my favorite.)

Quick Definitions

> *"No matter what people tell you,*
> *words and ideas can change the world."*
>
> —Robin Williams

Here are some terms and phrases that I will be using throughout the book. You are undoubtedly familiar with many of them. I share them here for contextual purposes—extending the typical definition to an 'AFP user' definition. No, there will not be a quiz at the end. Yes, they will keep us on the same page.

Types of Theatre Processes

Devised Theatre

Practitioners collectively improvise to create original stories for performance.

Ensemble Theatre

A collaborative practice that is used for both new and existing plays where all creative decisions are made collectively. Members of the ensemble play multiple roles throughout the process.

Applied Theatre

A performance-based medium for education and social development in a wide variety of non-traditional contexts and venues. The healthcare, business and social work arenas are popular application sites.

Drama Words

Stasis

The time of equilibrium in a story where things are normal and routine. This must be established clearly so when it is disturbed the problems of the story are clear. The desire to return to stasis feeds most story journeys. Typically, stasis is established in the beginning of the story and returned to at story's end. If the stasis is unchanged at the end, the story needs to be further developed.

Introduction

Like the first paragraph of a news article, this is the *Who, What, When and Where* of the story. The details of *Stasis* are shared here. This is a difficult portion of the story to make interesting as so much information needs to be shared here—always a wonderful creative challenge. The introduction ends when *Stasis* in disturbed by the...

Inciting Incident

The unique moment or action that disturbs the equilibrium disrupts the *stasis* and sets our primary character(s) off on their journey(s). Examples: The cyclone from the *Wizard of Oz*, Romeo and Juliet's first kiss, Simba sees his father Mufasa trampled to death in the *Lion King*.

Major Dramatic Question (MDQ)

The central story question that surfaces as a result of the inciting incident and fuels the journey of the primary character(s). The urgency of the journey is the desire to find the answer to the MDQ. "Will Dorothy ever return home?" "Can Romeo and Juliet be with each other for eternity?" "Can Simba become the King?"

Rising Action

The drive 'upward' towards the primary character's answer of the MDQ. It is referred to as 'rising' based on the Aristotle's traditional climactic structure of storytelling. This 'rise' begins the moment the inciting incident occurs and concludes when the character's MDQ is answered at the...

Climax

This is at the peak of the *rising action* where the MDQ is answered. This is typically the most emotionally heightened and importance-packed moments of the story as the primary character has now experienced a collection of intense experiences he/she has had to overcome to make it this far. These experiences or problems hindering the character's quest to answer the MDQ are called...

Obstacles

Anything and everything in the way of our primary character(s) smooth ride towards the answer of the MDQ. *Obstacles* can be human, psychological, natural, mystical or intellectual. We don't like smooth rides in stories. We LOVE problems—the more problems (obstacles) and the worse they are the better. We want our characters to suffer and earn their ascent to the *climax*. If Dorothy didn't have the wicked witch and flying monkeys to battle, we'd want our money back! We don't really want Romeo and Juliet to kiss and live happily ever after—we relish the viscous, bloody street fights of the Capulets and Montague's! We human animals crave the tension and conflict created by obstacles. Build your stories to be obstacle heavy. Because once the MDQ has been answered it's all downhill, or the...

Falling Action

This is the downward descent portion of our story after the MDQ has been answered. The falling action is typically obstacle free (or certainly obstacle light) as our primary character(s) must take what he/she/they have learned and return to stasis. While the falling action is typically illustrated in diagrams as equal in length to the rising action, this would be a story-building mistake and it is never so. Nobody wants to sit around and watch an enlightened character bask in his/her enlightenment. We do want to see how they will impact their stasis, but not for too long, and certainly not without some juicy obstacles. How they return to stasis also determines the genre of the story. If Romeo and Juliet are allowed to marry and live together in harmony, we call that a 'comedy' or simply a 'happy ending.' We know that our 'star-crossed' lovers return to stasis in a double suicide, which of course makes the story a 'tragedy.' Falling Action is important but needs to happen economically. Reminder: In contemporary films, which are, now limited to industry standards of less than 100 minutes, many 'falling actions' occur during the final credits. Yes, you got it...most people are walking to the parking lot during the *falling action* returning to their *stasis*!

Resolution

The unraveling of problems and events towards the solution of the primary character's problems once they have answered the MDQ. This typically happens along the *falling action* towards the return to *stasis*. Watching the primary character(s) 'put the pieces back together' and 'connect the dots' can be a smart technique for keeping the *falling action* entertaining and engaging for your audience.

Discovery/Revelation/Catharsis/Transformation

These are all new ideas that have been learned by the primary character(s) throughout their journey of the story. They are listed here in accordance with their values: Individual lessons learned that provide fuel for moving forward in the journey are called *Discoveries*. The collection of several *discoveries* together that provide access to new challenges and worlds along the *rising action* are called *Revelations*. The collection of several *revelations* that have granted access to the climax of the story where the MDQ is answered is called *Catharsis*. This is the highest and most densely packed emotional moment for our primary character where we see how the weight of the collected journey has impacted him/her/them in a way that is so profound it can be spiritually cleansing... the ultimate 'Aha!' moment. If the character accepts this giant lesson filled with *discoveries, revelations,* and *catharsis* he/she/they will have experienced a *Transformation*. This major change can be physical, psychological, social, spiritual, mental, etc. The character that accepts this *transformation* is eagerly speeds down the *falling action* and returns to *stasis* to excitedly share his/her/their new lesson. The character that refuses this *transformation* is destined for difficulty and we call him/her/them the Tragic Hero (See *Oedipus Rex*)

Arc/Journey

Marking the full experience of the primary character(s) throughout the story. The *journey* is often referred to as the *Dramatic Arc*; this can refer to the particular *journey* of the primary character(s) or the general movement of the entire story. When speaking in acting terms, directors often discuss the arc with actors to help trace the required growth and changes that occur within scenes, larger portions of the story (acts) or the entire story from start to finish.

Plot

The selection and arrangement of scenes taken from a story for the presentation to an audience. Important: *Plot* does not equal story. The story is the long form, the whole enchilada. The *plot* is what is essential, what is rung out of the story as we translate for performance. The story of Anne Frank hiding in Amsterdam transpires over two and half years. We cannot keep an audience in the theater for that duration of course. So, we must squeeze the *plot* out of the story to bring it to the stage. This is an important exercise and one we repeat often in our story-building processes. Life duplicated on stage is not theater. Life must go through several layers of editing, omitting, and transitioning before it becomes truth on stage. Realism is rarely truth in the world of Art.

Conflict

The collision or opposition of persons or forces in a play that give rise to dramatic action. As we have discussed, *conflict* is the driving force of all drama, all theater, and all stories. Four categories of conflict are typically presented: *Person vs. Person, Person vs. Nature, Person vs. God, Person vs. Him/Herself.* There are overlaps, exceptions and adaptations within these categories—they are not all encompassing, but they do provide a good place to start with students.

Protagonist

The primary character, group of central characters or force(s) in a story that the audience aligns itself with. This is the character(s) whose hand we are subliminally instructed to grab during the introduction and join (root, cheer, warn) for their journey towards their goals. It is interesting to note that while this term was originally created in connection with ancient Greek drama to single out the 'first' or 'main character in the play,' it's definition was broadened in the early 20th century to include 'the supporter of a cause.' This modern definition connects nicely with the ethos of AFP and worth sharing with your students.

Antagonist

The character, group of characters or force(s) within a story who actively opposes or is hostile to the protagonist(s). The antagonist's primary function is to provide obstacles between the protagonist and the attainment of his/her/their goals. From the Geek 'to struggle against' or to antagonize. The more formidable the antagonist the more difficult the protagonist's journey the more engaging the story. When the story becomes flat in rehearsal I always prompt our students to review what the antagonist is doing...probably not enough.

Contrasting Character

Placed beside the protagonist or antagonist, the *contrasting character* emphasizes their important qualities. These sidekicks emphasize important central character traits within the action of the story, thus alleviating the need to include in dialogue. i.e. To emphasize a protagonist's bravery the contrasting character is timid (Batman/Robin); to emphasize antagonist's intelligence the contrasting character might is dull minded (Frankenstein/Igor).

Opposing Forces

Those people or forces who are in conflict with each other through-out the story. My students usually give me a "duh" when we go over this one.

Balance of Forces

Each force must be equally and fiercely determined to reach their objectives. If one force (good or bad) is less committed to their objective, sufficient audience intrigue and engagement is lost; Translation: *Boredom.* In a football game we don't want to see a high school team compete against an NFL team. We don't like blowouts. We like to see fairly cast battles. We remain engaged when a *balance of forces exist.*

Acting Words

After teaching acting for over three decades, I have concluded that the work is extremely simple; this is why it's so difficult. 'Simple' is very difficult for us human animals to accomplish as we tend to apply unnecessary complexity to things we deem important. Acting students believe acting is extremely important therefore they read too many books and listen to too many experts who complicate the process with self-important blah-blah. There will always be 'acting gurus' who believe they have created the next amazing performance philosophy, only to be placed in a huge pile with all of the other next amazing performance philosophies. There are, to be sure, elements from several of these that are worthwhile—but these elements can all be traced back to the work of Constantin Stanislavsky, the father of acting training. He has several books that you'll find at the end of this book for further reading. After countless hours of acting training in studios and rehearsal halls, I agree wholeheartedly with a fundamental list of Stanislavsky essentials that make up all you need to know about acting. These terms are shared below. When students ask me "What type of acting do you teach?", I realize they are expecting me to share the vogue methods I prescribe to (i.e., Uta Hagen, Grotowski, Meisner, etc.) and are usually a bit flustered with my response: "There are two types of acting in the world: Good Acting and Bad Acting. I teach Good Acting." Good Acting includes the following:

Objectives

This is the goal or goals of the character in the story. They are categorized by time: *Immediate Objectives* are those the character is pursuing in the present moment (i.e., I want her to let me in the room.) *Scene Objectives* are those the character is hoping to accomplish by the end of each scene (i.e., I want her to kiss me.) The *Super Objective* is that one single, all encompassing, big goal the character is pursuing throughout the entire journey (i.e., I want her to forget her present life and run away with me forever.) *Objectives* must always be worded in the following format:

"I want (other character) to (do something)."

Objectives must always be about attempting to make another character physically do something. They should be simple and active. No actor ever won an award for how flowery they wrote their objectives. Good acting is a result of how they used those words as blueprints to getting what they wanted on stage, in the moment. Important: You cannot *play* an objective. Objectives are the goals that drive the action. The only (and I mean ONLY) thing an actor can actively *play* is an...

Actions

One-word verb used to accomplish an objective, Period. That's it. This is the simple part that actors try incessantly to complicate. Here's the most important acting lesson you and your students will ever need: We pursue *objectives* by playing *actions*. Simple, one-word verbs that an actor can play on another actor in order to get what they want (*objectives*). These one-word verbs need to be as active as possible—it helps to place 'To: _____" before the action. For instance, if the objective is 'I want her to let me in the room' possible *actions* to play to accomplish this *objective* are:

TO:

Knock

Scream

Request

Demand

Request

Squeeze

Tease

Trick

Flirt

You get the point. The choice of which *actions* to play is based on the circumstances of the play, the relationships of the characters and the moment at hand. It is better to be action-heavy than action-light. Stay away from passive actions (i.e., consider, think, understand, hope) that really cannot be played on another actor; a good rule of thumb is that if you can demonstrate the action with your entire body silently, it's a worthy action (i.e. slap, embrace, demand, beg). In our offstage lives, how many *objectives* do you think you pursue each day? Hundreds? Thousands? How many *actions* do you think you play each day? Thousands? Millions? Billions? How conscious are you of your objectives/actions throughout the day? Aha! The reasons we are unsuccessful offstage are the same reasons we are unsuccessful onstage. I often dream that we all behaved as well offstage as we do onstage. Alas, this is not the case.

The connections to acting well and living well are numerous and profound. That's another book.

Just to clarify the above, here's some Acting math:

Action + Action + Action = Immediate Objective

Immediate Objective + Immediate Objective + Immediate Objective = Scene Objective

Scene Objective + Scene Objective + Scene Objective = SUPER OBJECTIVE

That's it, take a bow, lights out, get ready to do it again tomorrow night!

Obstacle

Anything in the way of the character achieving his/her objective. This can take several forms: another character, another character's actions, an internal conflict, a natural disaster, supernatural occurrence, etc. Being the excellent reader you are, I'm sure you have already surmised that the more *obstacles* you have in a story the better. *Obstacles* create tension and tension creates audience engagement. Make your stories *obstacle* heavy. *Obstacles* are problems. What if Romeo and Juliet's families supported their love and committed to nurturing their marriage forever? There would be no *obstacles*, no play…no story. We need the 'ancient grudge' of the Capulet's and Montague's to justify the 'two hours traffic of our stage.' The *obstacles* between Romeo and Juliet's Super Objectives horrify, astound and sadden us. They also completely engage us in their story.

Subtext

What the character is thinking internally but not saying aloud. *Subtext* can also be called a character's *inner monologue*. Subtext is always happening in the character's mind—*Subtext* is the ocean, text (lines) are the boats.

Example: If the character's line (text) is "Hey, nice shirt!" and the subtext is "That's the ugliest shirt in the world" the line would be informed differently than if the subtext was "I wish I had that awesome shirt!" Try saying the same line twice but informed by the two different lines of subtext. (time for your acting debut) Welcome to acting! Consider the huge amount of *subtext* you experience in your offstage life everyday—all the thoughts that exist inside that your head—everything you think but do not say. Now imagine if you had to write down all of your *subtext*, or what you might refer to as your 'day dreams'—wow, right?!

#Breadcrumb Alert#

*Scientific dream studies have shown that an average daydream (subtext story) is about 14 seconds long and that we have about 2000 of them per day. In other words, we spend about half of our waking time or about one-third of our lives on earth spinning stories. We will dive more deeply into our brains and story science in **Program Note, Introduction: Why Stories?***

Magic 'If'

The *Magic 'If'* asks the actor to begin her/his work by asking, "What would I do if I were in these circumstances?" The answer to this simple question can be a springboard to creativity and inspiration because it allows the actor to realize the fact that, after all, she/he is living out a fictional life. It is the actor's job to make the fiction real to her/himself. By using the *magic 'if'* the actor is granting her/himself permission to accept this make-believe world in the same way a young child believes his doll is real, or she is really "Tarzan." It's *magic* of the kind that children possess and few adults retain from childhood. Acting training takes a page from a Buddhist proverb here, "All of life is a road back to childlikeness." Especially with the work of AFP story-building, since we create our stories ourselves, the importance of youthful *magic* cannot be overstated. Our process is more comfortable in a playground than a theater. Students tend to become quite solemn the closer we get to sharing our work publicly; it's the adult being caught in the dress up box. It's as these moments that I remind them that we are creating a 'play' not a 'serious.'

Important Acting Note: The ONLY thing and actor can play is an *action*. The only reason actors play *actions* is to accomplish their *objectives*. Actors cannot play objectives, obstacles, feelings, ideas or subtext; Objectives, obstacles, feelings, ideas and subtext all INFORM the actions. This may sound painfully simple and obvious, but you will see actors squirming and worming their way through rehearsals desperately attempting to play anything but a simple, one word verb called an *action*. There is a name for when actors play ideas other than *actions*: Bad Acting. Playing *actions* is extremely difficult because it's simple. Simple *actions* tend to reveal us in front of strangers. The human animal will do most anything to protect itself from being seen...from vulnerability. We will discuss how we create a safe story-building environment in future chapters—this is crucial. In the meantime, remind your students that 'Acting' is derived from the word 'Action.' If it were engaging to watch actors in thought we'd call public story sharing 'Thinking.'

Preparing the Story-Building Instrument

"Give me six hours to chop down a tree and I will spend the first four sharpening the axe."

—Abraham Lincoln

My students are regularly looking for the secret answers that will propel them into a life of guaranteed success. This is not unusual as the human animal is in constant pursuit of the easiest most painless paths. Suffering is indeed underrated and a life without pain is suspect. College takes four years for a reason. The 'magic' words I share with my students mystify them. They expect words like 'talent' and 'inspiration' I believe. Success in theater has little to do with talent—every person born has talent, just ask their parents. I have two packages of words that I share as the keys to success: Package 1: *Courage* and *Discipline*. If those two ideas are not embraced at every step of one's journey, they will never succeed. The *courage* to share one's story with strangers and the *discipline* required to make those stories meaningful are essential and in short supply today. Package 2: *Preparation, Preparation* and (you guessed it) *Preparation*. As Mr. Lincoln so clearly prescribes in the above quotation, the product of any event will never happen without appropriate preparation. We rehearse plays for six to eight weeks and perform them for two weeks. We research new medical advances for decades before they are introduced to the market. Creating a fine meal requires days of preparation and only a short time to consume. In a world with an increasingly fond appetite for immediate gratification, the lessons of preparation may be less popular than ever—they are also more important than ever.

I regularly curse Rene' Descartes as his iconic phrase "I think therefore I am" has caused a myriad of problems for our society as a whole; or perhaps less hyperbolically speaking, he has caused problems for college students. I have nothing but the utmost respect for Descartes as a philosopher and for his original intent of his famous quote. The problem surfaces with the contemporary sub-conscious connotation this quote carries: As long as I'm thinking, I'm fully participating in life; Not so! I have witnessed thousands upon thousands of people from every walk of life who are clearly thinking, but not living fully (See: Washington D.C.). What about the rest of who we are? I understand the importance of the brain and thinking, but that seems to be one-quarter of who we actually are. What about the body, the voice, and the spirit? In academia I tread the college campus alongside some pretty smart folks—just ask them, they'll tell you! How do they tread? Headfirst with that cumbersome, clumsy thing called a body being dragged behind. This is an important symbol of what we have become: Thinking machines. The work of story-building requires *doing*. My students love it (I think) when I implore them to get out of their heads and into their bodies by shouting "Stop thinking!" Can you imagine their confusion when a professor on a college campus demands they stop doing what they believe they should only be doing in college? Thinking is indeed an important part of the learning process, but not the entirety. (See: Contemplative Learning). Much of how we prepare our total instruments (body, voice, spirit, mind) for the work of story-building involves reminding the body that it is not only allowed to participate, it is *required* to participate. If we were to reword Descartes' quote to inform the work of AFP, it may be something like "I *breathe* therefore I am."

Study after study has proven that learning is accelerated when the content of the lesson is experienced rather than just memorized. Many educational experts would go further saying that real learning never happens during the rote memorization process. As you, I am sure, are aware, our current education system in the U.S. is stuck in an antiquated model that is unsatisfactory for today's students. I was as gentle and politic as I could possibly be with that statement. We are subjecting our students to a tortuous routine based almost entirely on convenience. This convenience made a great deal of sense during the Industrial Revolution where the intent of this new thing called public education was tasked with developing a population of factory workers to turn the wheels of the American Dream. The problem is we are not living in the 18th century nor are we in the midst of an industrial revolution. Our needs, habits, professions, economy, family structures, population...ok, EVERYTHING has changed about who we are educating but how we are educating them has not. Sir Ken Robinson, education philosopher and TED Talk sensation, heroically defines the sheer audacity of our present systems. He is an important voice with much to say—I highly advise some YouTube time with him. Among the many salient points he raises is our unwillingness to let go of our industrial model by continuing to teach children in "batches" by age when there is no shred of research that supports children learning best with similar aged students. In fact, all of the research suggests children learn best in mixed age groups. Mr. Robinson also points to the way we move and place students through the school building, in single file, silent lines down the hallways until they arrive at their holding center (class room) where they are assigned a seat in orderly, single file lines where complete silence is expected. This is a factory not a school. We could spend the rest of this book and several others discussing the current problems with Western education. Since you are probably a teacher and reading this book because you are well aware of systems inadequacies, let's just assume it's a given—our system does not need reforming, it needs **transforming**. I spend a great deal of time in Buffalo's middle and high schools. I see great teachers stifled by the restraints of the current system with regularity. You want out, I get it. For the purposes of our work in story-building, and more specifically the work of preparing the instrument in this section, I'd like to focus on two glaring results of the factory system negatively impacting our students:

1. The lack of physical freedom
2. The myth that silence is good

I am sure you have heard of this funny yet chilling parental anecdote: The first year of a child's life we encourage them to "Walk!" and "Talk!" with unbridled enthusiasm. The rest of their lives we tell them to "Sit down and shut up!" This leads to deeply entrenched beliefs that our stories do not matter. If we don't believe our stories matter, then we don't believe we matter. If we don't believe we matter, then we will surrender to the factory and guarantee we are not prepared to succeed in the world we live in. I'm getting extra serious here because its what I see in every middle school, high school, and college classroom I work in. Is there hope? You bet. The world we live in craves collaboration, diplomacy, creativity, diversity, innovation, physicality, intensity, identity, expression, intelligence, communication, exploration, ingenuity, bravery, and intense curiosity. Fortunately, these are all benefits and products of the story-building process. But before we can chop down that tree, we must sharpen the axe.

For the serious young actor, in-depth training in body and voice is essential. With the work of AFP, we never assume our students are all interested in being serious, professional actors. We do believe, however, that stories on stage should be delivered with quality performance standards. Too often social justice theater is given a pass on high performance standards. This is NOT the case with AFP. We believe students from all disciplines and interest areas can and should learn the core principles of good acting ('Good Living'). While I don't expect you and your students to attend a drama conservatory, I do expect core values of good acting to be learned and applied. We don't allow our Math/Science focused students to write sentence fragments or incomplete thoughts in English, right? Those students who are interested in pursuing a future in performance will find the skillset required in devised theater will enhance their overall acting skills in marvelous ways. We see our theater majors returning to traditional plays after their AFP work with improved acting skills time and time again, especially in the areas of courage, creativity, and focus.

AFP students-artists performing their original play LEVEL UP!

*"Creativity is the process of having original ideas that have value.
It is a **process**; it's not random."*

Sir Ken Robinson

Prologue III:
Process Highlights
(yes, this is the final prologue)

N ow that you have some context, I thought it best to shape this section as more of a list of reminders, than an extended narrative. My hope is that you'll be able to return to this section throughout the process to refresh your purpose. Our experience in the schools suggest that the systems in which teachers operate are often in direct opposition to the philosophies that drive the work of AFP. Don't get me wrong, we have encountered amazing schools with creative, inspiring and innovative learning environments; environments these schools have tirelessly assembled. More often than not, however, we see teachers who yearn for new, experiential pedagogy but find it difficult to assimilate new methods within traditional (how's that for a euphemism?) standardized environments.

Please allow this section to be the locker room before you go on the story-building field to play. My hope is the content here will act as your pre-game pep talk and remind you of why we are doing this work and how important it is to approach it each and every day with a clear mind and full heart.

- The primary objective of the work is to bring the content of the lesson from the **head** to the **heart** of the students. The primary vehicle for this transition is the **body**.

- Stop thinking, **Do**! Thinking and talking will only get you so far. Asking the student "How do you FEEL?" followed by "Show me with your body" will provide a road to truth and clarity.

- Story-building is hard work. Always refer to process as 'work.' This will intensify student focus and commitment while separating the work from preconceived notions as Story-Based Learning as frivolous or unimportant.

- Experiencing **feelings** is not only acceptable, it is *essential*. Encourage your students to **feel** and have them give words for those feelings. This completes a very important neural-path necessary for long-term learning. Do not allow students to make feelings precious—expect them, label them and they will soon be part of the village normal.

- The story building process is designed to be **flexible**, **fluid**, and **adaptable**. Use what works for your students in ways that work for your students. Don't try to replicate the AFP model by doing it 'right.' If you are actively and collaboratively processing the lesson (building stories) you are correct. This "right/wrong" is a leftover preoccupation from the industrial age.

- **Process** is the reason for everything. Every step of the work **is** the work. You the teacher are the process announcer— bravely share and surface lessons regularly with your students. Acts of compassion, forgiveness, conflict, division, anger, community, care and concern must be highlighted when they happen, or the students will never know what they are. These are tangible life skills.

- The collection of all lessons learned through the process is a collection of stories particular to each group of students; this collection of unique stories **is** the Story. Be on the lookout for reoccurring themes that surface in each group—be sensitive to this unique group pulse as it's the teacher's responsibility to make the students aware of their collective voice.

- The process is designed for the students to find their particular story each and every time. Don't assume you know what they want to share. You can guide the direction of the story for the sake of satisfying your learning objectives but be careful not to write their story for them. That would be *your* story.

- The product (the play) means nothing on its own—it is merely a brief expression of the group's story building process. It is always a good idea to have students share the process when sharing their final story performance with the audience. This is educational gold for administrators, faculty, staff, and student's families to witness the entirety of the process. This reflects college readiness and demonstrates multiple common core/state standard mandates.

- Story building does not require extra time. While it does require an initial schedule imposition to front load the work, the process actually becomes a time saver. This layered approach requires collaboration between multiple disciplines to build the story—thus, it is common to address English Language Arts, Social Studies, Political Science, Diversity, Geography and Literacy within one story building process.

- Always meet complaining with collaboration. Complaining stops the process of educating your students. Collaborating makes the multi-disciplinary work (above bullet) possible as we model this critical life skill for our students.

- Story building can be messy, and the process will get murky and frustrating. Two great questions to ask during these moments: "What lesson am I trying to teach my students with the story-building process?" "What lesson are my students trying to teach their future audiences with their story?" This will remove you from the anxiety of show product quality.

- There is no such thing as too much preparation or rehearsals. When collaborative groups complete assignments early, add more layers—if the village has met to work, everyone is working all the time until the closing circle.

- In the end, the story doesn't matter. The story is only a vehicle to teach your students the important lessons of **community building, conflict resolution** and **identity exploration**. The ultimate goals (Super Objective) are: 1) Your student's personal ownership of these tools so they can build healthy, strong, productive communities in their lives. 2) Your student's realization that they and their stories matter.

- **SAVE EVERYTHING.** Take photos of the boards, roll up large papers, collect your notes and student scribbles, save everything you and your students write down from the story building process...everything. Reserve and identify a special place in your room as the story-building library. You will resurface these elements as you create your story— this is the "gold." You may want to use an online project management tool (Basecamp, Smartsheet, Asana...there are many) as a way to organize, share and post the information in your story-building process. We have found these online management tools to be extremely useful and the students prefer to go paperless.

AFP Students perform their play then facilitate interactive workshop.

"That's what storytellers do.
We restore order with imagination.
We instill hope again and again."

Walt Disney

Program Note: Why Stories?

From the Shaman of Mesopotamia 7,000 years ago using chanted stories to communicate survival strategies to their tribes, to the masked chorus of Greek tragedies in 6th century B.C. who translated the complexities of the gods to eager Athenians, to the soul stirring Intore dance of Rwanda where Ignoma drums bring century old celebrations to us today—Story remains at the heart of who we are, how we communicate, and what moves us forward. Storytelling through performance helps us to process huge events into tangible entities—the indescribable becomes understood and the overwhelming becomes manageable. Through this lens, story becomes much more than a vehicle for entertainment. Story is and always has addressed a human need, often beyond our conscious control. We actually need story to help bring order to the chaos of our lives. We actually need story to provide structure and routine for the haunting randomness of our lives. Storytelling is the universal processing vocabulary of the human race. Story is the original social media.

Story: Brain Science

"Your brain has been evolutionarily hardwired to think,
to understand, to make sense, and to remember
in specific story terms and elements."—Kendall Haven

Like the many assumptions about 'theater' there exists a huge anecdotal cadre about 'stories.' It's no surprise when we hear how a great story engages, teaches, inspires and motivates its audience. We all know *that* stories have great power, but do we know *why* they do? Thankfully, due to the immense body of current brain science research conducted by neural and evolutionary scientists, cognitive psychologists and anthropologists, we do know why stories are packed with so much muscle. What does all of the research say? The simple answer: **Our brains are wired for story.** Kendall Haven's book *Story Proof: The Science Behind the Startling Power of Story* is an incredible marriage of neural science and storytelling that unveils the mystery of *why* we love, need and depend on stories. In Haven's research for his book he reviewed over 350 research studies from fifteen different fields of science. Every one of those studies as well as the studies they cite...*every single one*...agrees that stories are an effective and efficient vehicle for teaching, for motivating and for communicating factual and implicit information as well as abstract concepts. As the lone storyteller amongst 47 neural scientists, Haven was part of a recent research project sponsored by the U.S. Department of Defense (DARPA) to scientifically measure how stories exert influence. The results are breathtaking and fascinating! When I first read *Story Proof* I was like a kid in a candy store! Finally, loads of scientific evidence behind what us story/theater/drama folks have known forever...anecdotally. If I could take all of the audience, student, family responses of "This experience changed my life!" and magically translate it into scientific facts, I'd have a library of *why* stories work. But, I would never ask a neural scientist to build a story for performance, which is why they don't ask theater professors to conduct brain research. Thankfully, Kendall Haven's exhaustive work, has built a bridge between the art and science of story, a bridge built with the grey matter we all share, the human brain. I highly recommend reading his books, but here are some highlights to provide a scientific foundation for the work of building stories together:

- Over 150,000 years of story and storytelling have dominated human interaction and communication; and thus has evolutionarily rewired the human brain to think in specific story terms.

- Every culture in the history of this planet has created stories. Not all have created laws, written language or social codes—but all have created stories.

- The brain is predisposed to think in story terms: *To Understand, To Make Sense, To Remember*

- *To Understand*: Canadian researchers found a strong positive correlation between early storytelling activity and later math abilities (O'Neill, Pearce, and Pick 2004). It showed that learning story structure develops logical and analytical thinking as well as language literacy.

- *To Make Sense*: Most of what reaches your conscious mind is what neuroscientists call "Highly processed input" coming from the first sensory areas. This is where the subconscious mind first massages incoming information from the sensory organs (ears, eyes) and turns it into something that makes sense...*creating stories*.

- *To Remember*: Research by cognitive scientists has shown that "experiences not framed into story form suffer loss in memory." (Mandler 1984 and Mandler and Johnson 1977).

- The output of sensory brain regions is fed to the conscious mind for consideration—In other words, the brain converts raw experiences into *story* form and then considers, ponders, remembers, and acts on the self-created story, not the actual experience!

- Evolutionary biologists first proposed and developmental psychologists, biologists and neural scientists agree: 150,000 years of story dominance in how humans interact, communicate, archive and recall essential information has evolutionarily rewired human brains so that we are all born hardwired to think, understand, to make sense in and through specific story terms and concepts. This happens via the brain's *Neural Story Net*.

- **Neural Story Net**: A fixed, connected set of subconscious brain sub-regions that create and process specific story concepts and informational elements.

- *Neural Story Net* lies between external world and internal mind; distorts incoming information in order to make sense, thus the story created is not the story actually heard. Applying effective story structure minimizes this distortion.

- *Make Sense Mandate*: If the brain can't make sense, it won't pay attention. The brain has assigned the *Make-Sense Mandate* to the *Neural Story Net*, thus how effectively we tell stories is of vital importance as they determine the authenticity of the experience.

- Given that there is a specific portion of our brains dedicated to story, it is important to realize that there is no permanent area in the brain dedicated to reading and writing—these relatively new evolutionary activities must borrow from other areas of the brain to make them happen. People have been reading en-masse for a couple hundred years; people have been writing a cohesive language for about 7,500 years; people have been creating, sharing, and remembering stories for over 150,000 years.

Story: Life Simulators

"The storytelling mind is allergic to uncertainty, randomness, and coincidence. It is addicted to meaning. If the storytelling mind cannot find meaningful patterns in the world it will try to impose them. In short, the storytelling mind is a factory that churns out true stories when it can but will manufacture lies when it can't."
—Jonathan Gottschall

There are multiple important roles that stories play in our lives. This entertainment thing is relatively new, historically speaking. I am especially fond of the teaching potential of story. If you scrape away the embellishments, stories are merely vehicles for lessons. We will revisit this idea in detail when we discuss the creation of Themes in the story building process. However, for now, at the primal level we use stories to teach lessons. Mary Poppins convinced us that a 'spoon full of sugar makes the medicine go down," so too with stories; we personify evil with fire breathing dragons and illustrate wisdom with talking trees. We know the lesson will be sooner owned when wrapped in story. But why do we need so many lessons? Perhaps we are not as advanced as we would like to believe, and our basic impulse, our animal, needs story to survive? This is certainly a premise from another favorite book of mine, *The Storytelling Animal: How Stories Make Us Human* by Jonathan Gottschall. I love the universal themes and shared humanity Gottschall celebrates throughout this provocative book. Regarding stories as lessons "With most forms of popular story: mainstream films, network television, video games and genre novels, they're still structured on poetic justice—that's to say, the good guys still win out, and they do it by being honest and playing by the rules. Can it be that stories make societies work better by encouraging us to behave ethically?" He has a wonderful way of mixing human capacity and potential with self-deprecation and humor. "The future is a probabilistic simulation we run in our heads in order to help shape the world we want to live in. The past, unlike the future, has actually happened. They are reconstructions of what happened, and many of the details are unreliable. So, memory isn't an outright fiction; it is merely a fictionalization. We misremember the past in a way that allows us to maintain our protagonist status in the stories of our own lives. Our story evolves. Like a biological organism, it continuously adapts itself to the demands of its environment." *The Storytelling Animal* is an insightful, recommended read, and deeply supports several central commitments of my experiences and the work of AFP.

> *"Humans: the great ape with the storytelling mind."*
> —Jonathan Gottschall

Gottschall's poignant idea of how we use fiction as a *simulator* for life fascinates me and illuminates this book. Let's look at children at play. Play scholar Brian Sutton writes "The typical actions of orally told stories by young children include being lost, being stolen, being bitten, dying, being stepped on, being angry, calling the police, running away, or falling down. In their stories they portray a world of great flux, anarchy and disaster." While this may seem alarming at first glance, its actually quite clever and deeply engrained in all of us. Melvin Konner in his *The Evolution of Childhood* agrees, "Play across species helps youngsters rehearse for adult life. They are training their bodies and brains for the challenges of adulthood. They are building social and emotional intelligence." Gottschall takes this theory into adulthood as he analyzes the reasons for our passion for tragic, fictional stories, "Fiction is a powerful and ancient virtual reality technology that simulates the big dilemmas of human life. Fiction allows our brains to practice reacting to the kinds of challenges that are and always were most crucial to our success as a species." This need to practice and simulate tragedy, suggests evolutionary scientists, is an essential component to our survival. So important are these rehearsals that we, the story telling animal, won't take a break from our life simulators even when we sleep. Dream scientists suggest this is why our nightmares can become so scary, horrific and treacherous. These fictional tragedies in slumberland are actually more rehearsal time to prepare us for life's long list of potential dangers. These stories, like a flight simulator, allow us to take these dangerous rides and make mistakes without getting hurt. Imagine if they allowed Naval pilots to land on aircraft carriers in the middle of the ocean without practice?!? Evolutionary scientists ask the same question about navigating life's difficulties without the simulation of fictional stories to watch (and vicariously experience) while we are awake and sleeping—practice, practice, practice.

Story: Why We Rule the World

Historian and author Yuval Noah Harari (*Sapiens: A Brief History of Humankind*) contends that if it were merely about the nuts and bolts of survival, we wouldn't stand a chance against the chimpanzee. The chimp's ability to hunt, travel, escape and protect would far outlast ours on a deserted island. So why do we, homo sapiens, rule the world? Harari suggests two simple traits that separate us from our ape brothers:

1. Cooperation
2. Imagination

"Humans control the planet," he says, "because they are the only animals that can cooperate both flexibly and in very large numbers.

Now, there are other animals — like the social insects, the bees, the ants — that can cooperate in large numbers, but they don't do so flexibly. Their cooperation is very rigid. There is basically just one way in which a beehive can function. And if there's a new opportunity or a new danger, the bees cannot reinvent the social system overnight. Other animals, like the social mammals — the wolves, the elephants, the dolphins, the chimpanzees—they can cooperate much more flexibly, but they do so only in small numbers. The only animal that can combine the two abilities together and cooperate both flexibly and still do so in very large numbers is us, homo sapiens."

The reason for this exclusive cooperation hits to the core of our work in story building, "What enables us alone, of all the animals, to cooperate in such a way? The answer is our **imagination**. We can cooperate flexibly with countless numbers of strangers, because we alone, of all the animals on the planet, can create and believe fictions, fictional **stories**. And as long as everybody believes in the same fiction, everybody obeys and follows the same rules, the same norms, the same values."

I especially enjoy Harari's reflection on the possibility of other animals abiding by the same story principles we humans do, "All other animals use their communication system only to describe reality. A chimpanzee may say, 'Look! There's a lion, let's run away!' Or, 'Look! There's a banana tree over there! Let's go and get bananas!' Humans, in contrast, use their language not merely to describe reality, but also to create new realities, fictional realities. A human can say, 'Look, there is a god above the clouds! And if you don't do what I tell you to do, when you die, God will punish you and send you to hell.' And if you all believe this story that I've invented, then you will follow the same norms and laws and values, and you can cooperate. This is something only humans can do. You will never convince a chimpanzee to give you a banana by promising him, '... after you die, you'll go to chimpanzee heaven ... and you'll receive lots and lots of bananas for your good deeds. So now give me this banana.' No chimpanzee will ever believe such a story. Only humans believe such stories, which is why we control the world, whereas the chimpanzees are locked up in zoos and research laboratories."

Now, monkey business aside, Harari's story theory extends into extremely serious and important social contracts that we humans have seemed to not only accept but insist upon. Consider our story on the legalities of human rights, "Most legal systems today in the world are based on a belief in human rights. But what are human rights? Human rights, just like God and heaven, are just a story that we've invented. They are not an objective reality; they are not some biological effects about homo sapiens. Take a human being, cut him open, look inside, you will find the heart, the kidneys, neurons, hormones, DNA, but you won't find any rights. The only place you find rights are in the stories that we have invented and spread around over the last few centuries. They may be very positive stories, very good stories, but they're still just fictional stories that we've invented."

If you aren't already scratching your head, in awe of story power, consider our most widely accepted story of economics, "The most important actors today in the global economy are companies and corporations...like Google or Toyota or McDonald's. What exactly are these things? They are what lawyers call legal fictions. They are stories invented and maintained by the powerful wizards we call lawyers. And what do corporations do all day? Mostly, they try to make money. Yet, what is money? Again, money is not an objective reality; it has no objective value. Take this green piece of paper, the dollar bill. Look at it — it has no value. You cannot eat it, you cannot drink it, you cannot wear it. But then came along these master storytellers — the big bankers, the finance ministers, the prime ministers — and they tell us a very convincing story: 'Look, you see this green piece of paper? It is actually worth 10 bananas.' And if I believe it, and you believe it, and everybody believes it, it actually works. I can take this worthless piece of paper, go to the supermarket, give it to a complete stranger whom I've never met before, and get, in exchange, real bananas which I can actually eat. This is something amazing. You could never do it with chimpanzees. Chimpanzees trade, of course: 'Yes, you give me a coconut, I'll give you a banana.' That can work. But you give me a worthless piece of paper and you except me to give you a banana? No way! What do you think I am, a human?" So, what's the most amazing story ever written? *Romeo and Juliet*? *The Odyssey*? *The Bible*? Nope, says Harari, "Money, in fact, is the most successful story ever invented and told by humans, because it is the only story everybody believes. Not everybody believes in God, not everybody believes in human rights, not everybody believes in nationalism, but everybody believes in money, and in the dollar bill."

According to this theory, the reason we humans rule the planet is not because of our military might, our extreme intelligence or our even our capacity to love. Humans, Homo Sapiens, rule the world because we exist in a dual reality (objective and fictional) where it is possible to surface, create and share *stories* to define who we are and how we behave. Stories are the rules of our planet.

Stories + Education = Life. A Final Soapbox

The skillset used to build original stories is identical to those necessary for *conflict resolution, community building and identity exploration*. While current education trends may provide knowledge of how systems operate, they rarely provide tangible tools for students to navigate the complexities of their lives—the AFP story-building curriculum teaches skills and enhanced vocabulary that will impact the lives of students, their families, and communities. In short, instead of focusing on what they *know*, our methods focus on what students can *do* with what they know. This creative and collaborative process engages students in specific action steps that directly transfer to their lives as they build their lives... *their stories.*

Research, compromise, collaboration, discipline, creativity, compassion, innovation, and critical thinking are the core skills students develop. *We would never ask students to build a house without a hammer; we should never ask students to build their stories without the tools of story.*

This curricular vehicle is of particular relevance in our conflict-heavy global community and applicable to every subject and discipline. Whether a student is adapting to the emotional complexities of college life or climbing the daunting mountain of a family crisis, they are in desperate need of an expanded tool set to process their conflicted worlds in healthy, productive ways. The impact of conflict and struggle is not relegated to particular social classes, geographic locations or specific school subjects—the affluent and poor, the western and non-western, the sciences and humanities are all slowed by our increasingly conflicted world. This forced consumption is entering the minds and hearts of our students without an accompanying processing vocabulary thus creating huge obstacles in their ability to learn, grow and contribute. In short, the involuntary mass consumption of conflict has impaired a generation's ability to cope. *As future generations are provided with tools and vocabulary for story building, they are fueled to discover, define and share their identities. Multiple defined identities create strong families, communities, and countries.*

As we transition from knowledge-based communities to self-reflective, action-based communities the conviction that every human being, no matter how submerged in conflict, is capable of looking critically at their world in a dialogical encounter with others, and that provided with the proper tools for such encounter they can gradually perceive their personal and social reality and effectively deal with it. *When individuals participate in this sort of educational experience they come to a new awareness of self, a new sense of dignity; they are stirred by new **hope**.*

Students and Teachers Building Stories—Buffalo, NY (USA)

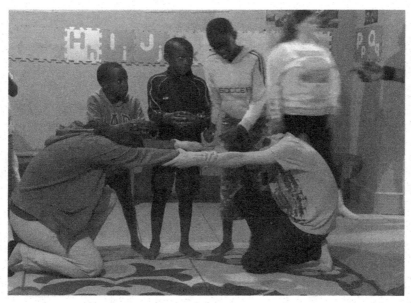

Students and Teachers Building Stories—Rwanda (Africa)

"I alone cannot change the world,
but I can cast a stone across the waters
to create many ripples."

Mother Teresa

The Story-Building Process
Act I: Building the Village

An anthropologist proposed a game to the kids in an African tribe. He put a basket full of fruit near a tree and told them that whoever got there first won the sweet fruits. When he gave them the signal to run they all took each other's hands and ran together, then sat in a circle enjoying their treats. When he asked them why they chose to run as a group when they could have had more fruit individually, one child spoke up and said: "UBUNTU, how can one of us be happy if all the other ones are sad?"

'UBUNTU' in the Xhosa culture means: "I am because we are"

If you have spent any time on Facebook, you are more than likely familiar with this simple, beautiful story. Ubuntu became the political philosophy of Nelson Mandela's leadership of South Africa. As the story goes, when Mandela was released from nearly three decades of wrongful imprisonment he looked into the eyes of his captors and said: "Ubuntu." In that context it is more than forgiveness, it is the realization that they, his captors, were in prison WITH him; by imprisoning Mandela they had, in fact, imprisoned themselves and all of humanity. Ubuntu is a very *African* idea that is difficult for our western minds to wrap around. When I bring students to Rwanda each year I tell them they will learn multiple important life lesson, but the most important one to bring home is "We before Me," also known as Ubuntu.

In North America we are raised from a very early age that individuality and our personal success is the priority. We are placed in a world of competition, each one for him/herself and may the best man/woman win. This ideal of self-promotion is often euphemized/justified as the 'American Dream.' What this 'dream' has in fact created are millions of people who practice "Me before We." This is contrary to our design—we are social animals wired to commune, communicate, and build communities. Ubuntu is more than unity or community...it is the ultimate releasing and accepting of the idea that we are truly and undeniably...One. This shared humanity is replicated in other cultural greetings beyond the Xhosa Ubuntu. From the Hindi and Sanskrit, the term Namaste' is used to acknowledge the divine in another. The lengthier translation of Namaste' is: I bow to the divinity in you. You bow to the divinity in me. When we are both in this place together, we are One. Wow, that's a powerful 'hello' right?! Rwandans greet each other in their native language Kinyarwanda saying, 'Muraho.' Muraho doesn't just mean 'hello,' it means "I celebrate your presence!" Another 'wow' right? What a beautiful way to greet each other—to celebrate another's existence in that moment. We have much to learn from our brothers and sisters across the oceans of the earth.

This is the energy and ethos we must create as we build our story-building villages. We use the term village instead of community in hopes of replicating the "We before Me" ideals of the villages we have visited in Africa. This can be a difficult transition for our American students. Think about our typical American greeting— Ubuntu, Namaste' and Muraho it is not. We typically look away from each other and throw a grunt in the general direction of our target without stopping—typical versions include: 'Wassup?' 'Hey,' 'How you doin?' With the subtext being "Please don't connect with me, I have things to do, whatever you do don't make eye contact." I share this not to condemn or belittle us American folk. I share this to illustrate the work necessary to bring our students (and ourselves) to the village. In order to build beautiful, engaging, meaningful stories we must listen, trust, respect, share, collaborate, compromise and contribute...*connect*. These characteristics are inside of each of us. Too often, we are not asked to practice these ideas, so they remain unfamiliar and dormant. Transitioning from the 'outside' or 'me' world to the 'village' or 'we' world can be a difficult, abstract task. We simplify and clarify this process by creating the **AFP Village Rules**.

The Village Rules are based on a similar idea from Boal's Theater of the Oppressed—the acknowledgement that we create a unified work ethic totally committed to the task at hand before the work can begin. This is essential. Like children, we all need and appreciate rules. Without rules we are allowed to behave badly. Also, like children, we might complain when given rules, but secretly we deeply appreciate the security resulting from the structure. Remember, *There can be no freedom without discipline.*

Remember, our ultimate goal of the warm-up is to gain a complete freedom of our story building instruments—our minds, bodies, souls and voices all available to respond to the creative impulse of the moment. We want our students to have this freedom, but freedom is earned through practicing the village rules. Think of these rules as the ten commandments of story building.

The Village Rules are created each time we begin a new process. They are created by the village and facilitated by the teacher. While ten is a good number to aim for, the village should decide the eventual total number of rules. I always suggest the teacher provides the first few rules—these are mandated, unchangeable and non-negotiable. These first rules provide the teacher with the opportunity to model the language and format the rest of the rules will follow. These first rules will also send a strong message to your student village: first, there is a leader in this process and secondly, the leader (school) has clear priorities.

> #Breadcrumb Alert#
>
> *People often confuse strong, collaborative environments with democracies. This is completely untrue. Democracies, where everyone gets equal say and there is no lead voice, always create unclear, ineffective products on stage. The group might 'feel good' existing in their reborn Woodstock, but that feeling never reaches the intended audience. Democracy kills the creative structure crucial to building meaningful stories. The lunatics cannot run the asylum— the teacher is boss, or as my dear mentor Broadway legend Andre' De Shields called himself when teaching, the 'Benevolent Dictator.'*

Here is an example of the Village Rules from a recent AFP story building process created by the village and its teacher:

- We agree that Story is first.

- We agree to respect each other as collaborators and as people.

- We agree that our intention is to help each other tell the best possible story together as a community.

- We agree to send messages and requests through appropriate channels.

- We agree to evaluate each other by asking questions whenever possible, rather than making conclusions or delivering orders.

- We agree to consider anything for five minutes.

- We agree to discuss our differences with each other as they surface.

- We agree that we cannot do it alone and that we need each other.

- We agree that self-deprecation of any kind will provide obstacles in our work.

- We agree that a loving, caring, nurturing village is the foundation for our success.

You will note that the first three rules were created (mandated) by the teacher. These were essential and non-negotiable to me. As you build the village rules there should be plenty of time to unpack the reasoning behind each rule. Encourage the students to ask questions and demand clarity. Be ready to explain why you believe the first few rules are important. We never number the rules as this would imply importance and priority. Each rule is as important as the rest. The village should determine the order of the rules, as one rule might flow better in one place than another—like a story. Encourage the village to be particular about language and word usage. Like each student, word choice matters deeply. As you build the village rules it is an opportunity to model the process that lies ahead—you are rehearsing the story building as you build the village rules. For instance, if one student is especially quiet during this process, ask them directly for input. After they have shared an idea publicly celebrate that student's input, which will model inclusion for the village. I always make a controversial suggestion to include in the village rules to entice student feedback. Something like "We agree that secrets will help the process." The students will explode in disagreement, and you will agree to strike that idea from the rules. You have modeled compromise and the students have taken a step towards ownership of their village.

Spend time on the village rules. Encourage diverse opinions. Constantly and explicitly remind the village of how important these rules are. Edit, tinker and change the wording until the village feels it is perfect. Allow for healthy debates between individual students—again, these are modeling opportunities for healthy collaboration. Practice the village rules as you create the village rules. Finally, develop a procedure for how the village will hold each other accountable practicing the rules during story building (class) time. These procedures should, again, reflect the Village Rules and be very *village-rulesish* in their application. I am sure you are becoming increasingly aware of important realities of the story-building process: Everything matters, and we are always practicing the utopian ideals of AFP; thus the process becomes the incubator to practice and refine behaviors that will eventually be the responsibility of the each student to share with their future villages. While I would love for all my students to practice these collaborative ideals every moment of their lives, I only have control of them during our scheduled meeting times. I can't follow each of them around all day, every day. So, I tell them once they walk into the room (theater, studio, etc.) it is time for village rules, it is a class requirement. You will find they will feel so proud of these rules that they will be attempting share them with their other communities...this leaking is great news. We want them to feel so strongly about their work that they must share it with others... this is kind of the whole point, right? There is nothing like the zeal of the convert.

The final rule (or something like it), *We agree that a loving, caring, nurturing village is the foundation for our success*, is crucial. This rule always allows me to voice how serious I am about their treatment of each other. Loving each other is not optional; it is a class requirement, it is an *assignment*. This always opens the way to a healthy village discussion about loving, caring and nurturing. Students typically have very little experience with useful definitions of these words that are applicable to their lives. They report surface definitions exported from popular culture, social media and Hollywood. They report a history of being told these words are 'hush-hush' and not to be discussed in school. They report unhealthy family obstacles to honestly understanding these words. Overall, they report a general dissatisfaction with their present definitions of these words and welcome the village opportunity to redefine them as they 'should be.' Most importantly for the teacher, this conversation will surface personal feelings from the students about important issues that touch their hearts. These conversations will accelerate their relationships with each other, provide important scaffolding for their village and set the bar for exploring high-staked content. Every effective story contains high-staked content (see 'Conflict') so conversations like this model the work ahead of the village—they are, quite literally, rehearsing (simulating) content worthy of story. Contemplative Learning places an emphasis on the use of emotionally charged language in classrooms as an important piece of the whole education pie. When and why did it become taboo to wrestle with emotions and feelings in school? Your student's lives will be jam packed with emotional experiences and lightly sprinkled with fact memorization—this is important stuff! You may find these high-staked conversations awkward and uneasy to navigate initially. That's expected and understandable—its not typical of most student experiences. However, as you move forward through the term, this content will eventually feel routine and expected in the process. Emotions and feelings are not precious abnormalities to run from, they are natural parts of being human. How you, the teacher, facilitate these less familiar roads for your students will provide important vocabulary for their future bumpy life rides. You will undoubtedly be stretched and uncomfortable—that's important for your students to witness. You are human too, right?

#Breadcrumb Alert#

I was once responding to questions after I delivered the keynote address at a national education conference when a student approached the microphone with a strong spine and furled brow, "I'm passionate and completely obsessed with teaching language literacy. It's what I have been studying for years, it's what I want to spend my life teaching, developing and researching. I just want to teach my future students what I know and am not interested in being their mother, sister, aunt or confidante…What's your suggestions?" My suggestion was simple, "Don't be a teacher." Perhaps historically it was appropriate to remain emotionally distant for our students so they could focus on the content at hand? Perhaps the defined rules inherent in education systems derived from religious institutions mandated this separation?

> *Regardless, I firmly believe the definition of teacher is much wider now than ever. I would go so far to say it's the responsibility of teachers to provide skills for processing life regardless of discipline. I'll go one step further: Our particular disciplines (i.e. English, science, math, social studies) are merely vehicles for what all teachers should be primarily teaching: Tangible life tools and vocabulary to assist our students in navigating the complex world that awaits them. I have seen too many students from 'great schools' with no life tools and massive debt. Teachers widening their instruction net can contribute to the solution of this huge problem.*
>
> *It requires three things:*
>
> 1. *Training*
>
> 2. *Courage*
>
> 3. *Discipline*

The 'Kumbaya Effect'

With all of this emotional openness I am encouraging you must be wondering: What if this gets out of hand? How can I prevent my class from becoming a free-for-all therapy session? Good questions—-really good questions. Like anything introduced in the classroom you must provide clear **objectives, structure, and clarity.** The first emotionally charged conversation is the opportunity to convey these rules. Diving into these conversations without structure is like stepping on an algae-covered stone in a raging river—you will lose your footing, fall into the water and be swept away by the current grasping for land. No control = Teacher Hell. You must provide the 'Whys' for your students:

- **Objective:** We are engaging in this adult conversation to examine these issues as they will be important for our story and for your lives. I will be highlighting important tools and vocabulary during this conversation that might help you.

- **Structure:** We must practice our Village Rules during this conversation (Read them aloud together—make it public and current). It is important that you know the Village Rules are here to create a safe environment for each of us. If you ever feel unsafe, please let me know. We must agree that what is shared here is not for the rest of the school— Village Rules. As we move through this conversation I may ask you questions—these will help us stay on our objective and make the best use of our limited time together.

- **Clarity:** We are opening this conversation to the Village in order to accomplish our objectives. You are not obligated to speak but everyone must be present. This is not therapy, but discussing emotions and feelings can be therapeutic. If you feel emotions that surprise you that's OK—its normal to feel things, its what makes us human. If someone becomes sad, please don't ask them to stop being sad or begin singing 'Kumbaya.' Feel free to comfort your fellow villager, but don't ever allow any sad student to leave the village. We would never try to escape if someone began to laugh. Emotions are important but not precious. I always remind students that they weren't born laughing—they were born crying…loudly! When they first cried everyone in the delivery room cheered—another reminder of the importance of our child history.

After you have defined the **objectives, structure and clarity** there will be a shape for the conversation. It's OK that this takes time—never rush through any of this. The content of these meaningful conversations IS the content of the village's story. The skillful teacher is always collecting this content throughout the process. I have found that nothing meaningful and worthwhile in story building and life happen quickly. Please, please, please fight the urge to rush through the preparatory aspects of story building to get to the next step. The preparations ARE the building blocks of the story.

Special Note: You will undoubtedly experience unexpected emotions from your students during this process. In AFP, we always imagine each student we meet is struggling with something. These struggles eclipse all socio, economic, cultural and assumed barriers—ALL people are struggling, their pain is real, and one person's pain is not greater than another's—pain is pain. Some of these struggles may be triggered by the work of story building. It is important to use your teacher radar to decipher which emotional issues can be dealt with by you, their teacher, confidante, aunt, mom, and which emotional issues should be directed to someone in your organization trained to manage these issues. **School counselors, social workers, psychologists, and therapists should all be important partners with you and your work.** We never bring the work of AFP to a school without their counselors/psychologists present. You know your students best—it is important that you collaborate effectively with your local mental health resources to provide the best support system possible for your students. School counselors are always appreciative of the 'heads up' and becoming aware of a student issue they may never had known about had it not surfaced with the story building work. School counselors never appreciate being pulled in late in the process—prevention is best.

On the flip side, we have been involved with schools where the counselors were overzealous and over prepared the students for a 'traumatic experience' before the work ever began. While well intentioned, these professionals actually triggered traumatic experiences that may or may not have ever occurred if we allowed the students to have their own experiences without the daunting warnings. It's a fine line here that, in my opinion, becomes the reason why many teachers fear this work (See: Courage). This is an important line to walk and here's a simple suggestion that has proven highly successful for the past decade with the work of AFP: Identify the local mental health resources in your school or organization. Communicate the **objectives, structure, and clarity** of the story-building process with these resources. Create a collaborative plan to assist students should that be come necessary. The vast majority of AFP story-building processes have never had a need for using outside mental health resources. What has been more common are the countless mental health professionals who thank us for providing challenging experiences for their students; experiences that surface discussions they would not have had otherwise. Many of the 'point people' at the schools we regularly work with are counselors and psychologists. AFP has become an annual expectation for these mental health professionals to such an extent that they request themes they'd like us to address in future visits. As you can see, it is essential to put the mental health support pieces in place before every process.

#Breadcrumb Alert#

New York State Education mandates the Dignity for All Students Act (DASA). NYSED states: "New York State's Dignity for All Students Act seeks to provide the State's public elementary and secondary school students with a safe and supportive environment free from discrimination, intimidation, taunting, harassment, and bullying on school property, a school bus and/or at a school function." Signed into state law in 2010 DASA requires that each school in New York provide "...instruction in civility, citizenship, and character education by expanding the concepts of tolerance, respect for others and dignity to include: an awareness and sensitivity in the relations of people, including but not limited to, different races, weights, national origins, ethnic groups, religions, religious practices, mental or physical abilities, sexual orientations, gender identity, and sexes." New York State is not alone in responding to the dangerous bullying epidemic that blanketed (and continues) our schools with mandates, laws and proposals. The trick is finding meaningful programming to fulfill these mandates—everyone wants anti-bullying programming, not everyone knows how to provide it. AFP's work in the schools directly satisfies the DASA requirements—that's intentional. I urge you to find your state's anti-bullying requirements, as they will help you to justify the work of story building. A student from a school in Buffalo came to us beaming after an AFP performance and workshop, "That was awesome and nothing like I expected!"

"What did you expect?" I asked.

She replied, "You know, the typical no-bullying assembly where someone stands up and yells at us about how dangerous bullying is." "You mean someone bullies you about bullying?" one of my students asked, "Exactly!" replied the young lady.

Lastly, once the village has agreed on the rules, post them prominently and publicly on the wall of the room. They need to be large and obvious enough that villagers can refer to them at any time. Village rules can be modified as the process moves forward. That is the history behind the rule, 'We agree that self-deprecation of any kind will provide obstacles in our work.' We had a particular villager who suffered from deep insecurities whenever she spoke publicly. We knew this because she always preceded her comments with 'This is stupid, but...' or "I don't know, but..." The rest of the village soon became frustrated with her constant belittling of herself—they had decided that her self-deprecation was unfair to her, thus unfair to the village. They took a stand and added the village rule with a physical addition: Each time anyone self-deprecated, they were mandated to stop, physically spin around in a circle, erase the insecurity and proceed confidently. This girl (dizzily) worked through her insecurity and became empowered to share her thoughts later in the process. The village at work. Here's another example from a recent class:

Village Rules

(Based on the work of Augusto Boal's Theatre of the Oppressed)

- We agree that Story is first.

- We agree that these rules are ideas that must be activated in word and action.

- We agree that we respect each other as collaborators and as people.

- We agree that our intention is to help each other tell the best possible story together as a community.

- We agree to support each other's creativity.

- We agree to respect each other's rehearsal and preparation time.

- We agree to send messages and requests through appropriate channels.

- We agree not to re-write or re-do another's work.

- If there is a concern, we agree to discuss it with the original collaborator.

- We agree to evaluate each other by asking questions whenever possible, rather than making conclusions or delivering orders.

- We agree to evaluate and discuss changes in ways that are respectful and encourage creative thinking.

- We agree to consider anything for five minutes.

- We agree to discuss our differences with each other as they surface.

- We agree that we cannot do it alone.

- We agree that we need each other.

- We agree that self-deprecation of any kind will provide obstacles in our work.

- We agree that a loving, caring, nurturing village is the foundation for our success.

- We agree to present a unified, supportive leadership to the entire community.

- We agree to represent our village in word and action.

- We agree that Story is first.

Once the Village Rules have been written in stone it is time to move the creation of the village from the brains to the bodies of the students. This is a sequence you will repeat multiple times throughout the process: *Think on your butt, act on your feet*. There should never be a brain-focused discussion that simply stops at discussion's end. The brain introduces the idea, the body makes the idea into truth. Ideas that seem amazing in discussion often lose their shine when introduced to the body. This is a crucial lesson: Thinking is an important first step to the nurturing of ideas, but never the entirety of the idea. The body must be involved for the entire cycle of learning to be complete. Here's an extremely simple teaching recommendation: At any moment during the creative process when you are unsure of your student's sureness (i.e. thinking) provide the following direction: 'Stand up and show me so we all understand.' These impromptu rehearsals activate the thinking and will require the students to use each other to fully bring the thoughts out of their heads and on to the stage (i.e. you be the mountain, you be the giant). This is the magical bridge all ideas must walk across during the AFP story building process. We call this transition from the head to the body 'finding the truth.' The villagers engage their truth vehicles, their instruments, in the circle each time you come together. The Village Rules become truthfully and authentically owned in the circle during the AFP warm up.

Activating the Village: The AFP Warm-Up

We begin and end our work in a circle each time we meet. This circle represents the physical formation of our 'Village' in the Anne Frank Project. The circle also represents the oldest story sharing shape there is. Mandated by the need for warmth and light, tribes, clans and nations gathered to conclude their days in circles surrounding the fire. There, amidst the dancing flames, magical stories were exchanged. These were not entertainment stories... these were **survival** stories. How did the hunt end? Why does the mountain spew fire? How can we grow more food? How can we protect ourselves from intruders? These are a few of the possible

MDQ's from our Mesopotamian ancestors. Thus, the circle is more than a shape in AFP land—it is the sacred ritual that initiates and concludes our work together each time we meet as a village. You will find that your students will crave this routine. Teachers we train regularly share how the circle provides important kinesthetic 'book ends' to each day's work in class. We know that engaging the whole student (body, voice, spirit, mind) is an important factor to their learning success. The physical warm-up work in the circle is fun, easy and flexible. In this section we will explore, in detail, the many exercises, games and physical routines that can happen within the AFP circle as *you bring your students to the village.* Below is a short overview of why we do this work.

Breath: The Foundation

Here's how ideas become voiced thoughts: The motor cortex of the brain sends a signal down the spinal cord, through your central nervous system to make in your abdominal area for breath to support the thought-the size of the breath is in direct correlation to the size of the thought. Your body instinctively moves your guts around to accommodate the space needed for breath.

Why so much fuss about the breath? Because breath IS thought. Try this: Count out loud to 5. Now count out loud to 20. Notice you didn't have any extra breath for 5, nor did you run out of breath for 20. Why? Because breath = Thought. Let's continue the breath's journey from idea to voiced thought—thoughts are articulated into words—words multiplied are complex thoughts, also known as sentences—multiple sentences combined from a variety of sources are stories.

There are mountains of research explaining and unpacking the importance of breath. Breath is the essence, the source for everything...literally everything. The ancient traditions and practices of meditation, prayer and mindfulness all begin and end with breath. I have shared many books and research studies about breath in this book's resource section.

Body: The Vehicle

Our central nervous system works together in complete harmony with our involuntary muscular system to counteract gravity. Read that again. This is a fancy way of saying we don't have to do anything to stand up right. Our bodies are amazing achievements designed to accomplish some spectacular things. The problem arises when we don't trust, or realize, this design. Reread the first sentence of this paragraph again. Our bodies should hang freely from our skeletons supported by complex mechanisms and neural communications we don't need to worry about. We need to do what is so difficult for us to do: *Nothing*. Most people mistrust this design by using their voluntary muscular system to hold themselves up in space. As we know, the involuntary muscular system and our central nervous system have already agreed to take care of that for us. So, the result is...Tension! Tension is trapped energy—energy that can be used in much more productive ways (like sharing stories with an audience!). Our voluntary muscular system is designed for one thing only: Movement! When we use this system to assist another system unnecessarily, its native mission, movement, is stifled. In story-building we NEED our bodies to become mountains, antelopes, houses, emotions, and explosions. In story-building our bodies literally ARE our tools...for everything. When we move from the paper to the stage in our work the students always ask if we can have the special props they wrote in their stories. They are imagining pyrotechnics and real trees. My response is always the same, "you can have whatever you want in the entire universe on stage in your story—you just have to make it with your bodies and voices." So, if our voluntary muscular system is busy holding our bodies up in space, it will not be available to respond to the creative, physical, constant demands of story-building; thus, the story and your student's passions will be diminished. The impulse to naturally respond to the moment will be lost, and as a result truth will be lost, and when truth is lost audience engagement is lost. This is crucial village work and clear justification for why we do a physical warm-up in the circle. The students will see the circle work as fun and the way they get ready for the village—how they 'punch in' to work. Beyond this, you will know there is serious rewiring going on inside your students where the emphasis on the brain is being redirected and shared with the rest of the body. You will witness firsthand the shift from your students *thinking* to *doing*, working from their *heads* to their *hearts*. I don't share this anatomy lesson with third graders, I share bits and pieces with high-schoolers, I share it all with college students. You know your students best, it's up to you. If I were a biology teacher, this is a cool way to deliver some content.

#Breadcrumb Alert#

By now you may have realized that the requirements for building stories are really just thinly disguised skills for life. Education uses the term 'soft skills' when talking about things like breathing, speaking and collaborating. I call them 'life skills,' they are anything but 'soft,' and vital for all our students if they are to navigate the complexities of their worlds with any success. Learning about your body, its design and potential seems important to me. Collaborating, resolving conflicts, and exploring identities are also important to me and are taught throughout our process. In the end, I don't care about the final story. I care about the skills the students have acquired throughout the process. This book is here to help you identify and celebrate those skills when they surface with your students during the process.

Note: Every time the ensemble commits to the process and cares less about the final product, the final product is outstanding; every time the ensemble is product driven, the final product suffers. Every time; No exceptions.

Voice: The Revealer

Like acting, there are several approaches to training the voice. I was fortunate to be trained in the Linklater technique in graduate school. Kristen Linklater wrote one of theater's 'bibles' of voice training, *Freeing the Natural Voice,* where she states, "This approach to voice is designed to liberate the natural voice and thereby develop a vocal technique that serves the freedom of human expression. To free the voice is to free the person." We include the voice in our warm-up routine because the voice is the ultimate revealer of self. Students are typically braver with their bodies than their voices—sharing the voice can be vulnerable. Most of us speak in a voice that is covered in some way to protect ourselves from being known. There are many social injustices about the voice fixed in our student's minds: *If you talk like _____ then you are a _____*. Fill in the blanks with multiple unfair, hurtful assumptions. Another reason for including voice in the warm-up is the reminder that everyone' story (voice) matters. Some of the exercises include a brief sound to accompany a movement—that's the student's story in that moment! These sounds, grunts and laughs are the building blocks to story, the atoms that will multiply to become full bodied stories. We must begin simply. It is important as teachers to be on the lookout for philosophy reinforcements like these during the circle warm-ups. This routine is filled with opportunities to remind your students how much they and their stories matter. This is also important foundation building as the student's 'voices' will be essential as you build your story—you need their input at every turn. The circle is where you plant those seeds. Like the body, the voice needs a shot of freedom and permission to play. That's the focus of the voice work in the warm-up.

Mind: The Present

Have you ever watched a live performance and one performer stood out from the others? You couldn't quite put your finger on why, but you were drawn to them for some mysterious reason. There is no mystery. The reason you couldn't take your eyes off that one performer is simple:

Presence. This idea has evolved into a magical quality one is either born with or not. I used to prescribe to this idea—that you can't teach Presence, either you got 'it,' or you don't. I was clearly young and naïve, as I now know for a fact that you can teach and learn presence. Like other simple ideas we have discussed, this is by no means an easy task. Presence means being completely alert and attentive in the moment we describe as 'now,' or the present. We all spend a great deal of time in our heads, spinning stories that may be 'truthy' as narrative neurology experts like to say, but not necessarily 'truthful.' If you are like any human animal I have ever met, you spend most of your thought time in two places you have no control of: the past (regret) and the future (worry). These are the performers you are not drawn to on stage, or in life. Most of us spend the least amount of time in the now, in the present. Those who do, we are drawn to on and off the stage. This is not just a mental idea, although it begins there. The *Presence* work of the AFP warm-up focuses on getting the body, voice, mind, and spirit into the now—the Present. My students recognize this portion of the warm-up as 'getting right' with themselves and their story-building community; part of the necessary 'punching in' so we can get to work. Important stuff.

Spirit: The Child

Quite simply: We are too serious! The idea that we should 'stop behaving like children' and 'grow up' is instilled in us from, ironically, a very young age. We are fed a false promise that being an adult is good and being a child is bad. For all of us who fall into the adult category we know this to be a great mystery and long for the days of child's play. Our inner child lies dormant in most of us, waiting for a chance to surface—isn't it mind-boggling that we are waiting for an invitation to play? Some of us wait for so long that it becomes difficult to remember how to play. This is the job of a theater professor, to return our students to that place of eternal curiosity, physical freedom and naïve playfulness. The Buddhists know that 'all of life is a road back to childlikeness.' I never claim to teach my students how to play, rather my job is to *remind* them of where they've already been—in the sandbox, on the playground and under a blanket tent making silly sounds. This all may sound easy—think again. We find in the work of AFP story-building that this is consistently the most difficult part of the warm-up. Why? It is vulnerable and unveiling to let others see you being silly. We spend a great deal of time and energy each day protecting ourselves from being seen. Our physical and emotional armor, we believe, protects us from those outside forces who, once they see us, will hurt us. I don't share this with a spec of sarcasm...I know it's real because I see it every day. Our serious armor may indeed protect us from outside forces, but it also prohibits free breath, honest expression, and open collaboration, three vital components of story building. You will find that this is the optimal modeling opportunity as a teacher. If you passionately squawk and fly about the room like a giant bird, your students will too. Not only have you made it cool to play, but you have also set the bar for bravery and the importance of full commitment; there is no 'kind of' in good acting, either you are fully committed, or you are not. Commitment is a key lesson to cement into the village during the warm-up and the free spirit is the best vehicle for this. Actors during Shakespeare's Elizabethan period were called 'players.' As multiple child psychologists reiterate in their research, play is hard work! While freeing the silly spirit is a difficult task, especially amongst self-conscious adolescents, it is an invaluable tool for the work ahead. It is not a free for all either—we don't just count to three and ask our students to be silly...there are practical steps and exercises that this book will share with you. A simple truth to keep in mind is that we always know when the childlike spirit of the village has been attained: the room is filled with uncontrollable smiles.

The goal of story building preparation is individual and group freedom; It's not magic, it's hard work! An ancient proverb found in multiple global communities (one of my favorites) seems appropriate here: *'There can be no freedom without discipline.'* As we engage the body, voice, mind and spirit in the preparation for story building (the warm up) please be aware that no matter how silly, how fun and how irreverent the exercises may seem, there is always a **reason** for everything we do. Your students can look forward to the fun—you, their teacher, their guide, must remain several steps ahead of them in total clarity as each step really is a brick in the story you are building. As you move forward, if you cannot remember the reason for a particular exercise return to this book for assistance. If you still cannot locate the reason, don't do the exercise anymore. Repeating something 'just because' will often stop rather than fuel the process. Look for the smiles and be mindful of your objectives in the preparation process.

Following is a pictorial and video overview of AFP's most popular warm-up exercises and circle work sequence—there are many more.

While the variety of exercise will vary the sequence is the same as we prepare the instrument and clarify the village: Access low breath, engage the body, open the voice, extend the body and voice together, activate village rules by sharing, connecting and depending on each other. Have fun…it's essential!

Initiating the AFP Circle Sequence in the U.S. and Rwanda

The following AFP warm-up overview is illuminated by the playful sketches of Eve Everette, former Buffalo State/AFP student and staff member.

AFP Village Building Warm-Up and Exercises

WARM UP

CIRCLE UP - "LET'S GET HERE"

Practice:

- Form a circle
- Feet under hips or slightly outside
- Hold hands
- First breath: leave external distractions outside
- Second breath: get present with group
- Third breath: Choose a risk to take or something to improve*

Benefits

- Builds focus, presence, community, trust, and responsibility
- Allows time to introduce prompts such as quotes, images, stories, and photos that infuse the day's work.

Questions

- Why do we circle up?
- What does the shape allow us to do?

*Wrap it in breath: you can't go back on it. You promised yourself and the village that you'd do it.

BREATH & BODY

Breath is a vehicle for voice. We need low, supported breath to tell strong stories

Practice

- Let hands drop
- Stand with feet under hips and get balanced
- rock to toes
- rock to heels
- rock to outside of left foot, then right foot

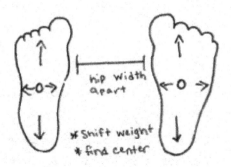

Imagery:

- Grow a root in the arch of foot into the Earth
- Let belly hang - we need space to breathe! (Think Buddha belly)
- Find Chi - two fingers below belly button. This is our energy source
- Breathe into Chi - Bellow should balloon out like a crying newborn baby

- Take three deep breaths in through the nose and out the mouth. Keeps eyes open and alert.

Benefits

- Gets us out of our heads and into our body
- Connect to Earth, grounds us
- Creates space for low breath
- Calms body and mind

Questions

- Where is your center, your energy source?
- Where do our stories live?

SOFT KNEES LONG SPINE

After planting our feet, let's allow our spines to lengthen and our knees to bend.

Practice

- Imagine a helium balloon is attached to the top of your head lifting you up.
- Imagine a sandbag is tied to your coccyx (tail bone), pulling your pelvis under, allowing your lower back to relax.
- Let your belly hang
- Breath into your Chi (inhale through nose, exhale through mouth)
- Lengthen on exhale.

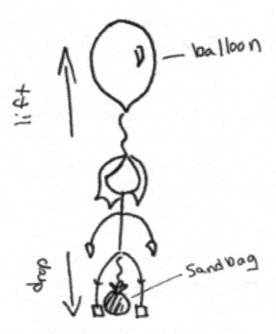

SHOULDER CIRCLES

Practice

- Pretend there is a drawing tool (pen, pencil, paintbrush, etc.) attached to the end of your shoulders.
- Draw small circles forward, then backward
- Draw large circles
- Involve whole body, bending at the knees
- Try opposite rotations
- Flip palms (one down, one up) and follow them

Benefits

releases tension and stress in upper body (any crunchy sound is fascia, your cushiony-connective tissue, opening up.)

Questions & Comments

- What colors are you drawing?
- Are you breathing?
- Let sound come out while you make circles

ROLL DOWNS

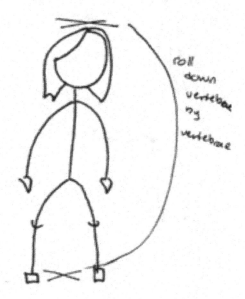

roll down vertebrae by vertebrae

Practice

- Start in long spine, soft knees
- Snip "balloon" and let head drop

- Follow crown of head, vertebrae by vertebrae, until hanging at waist. Keep knees soft
- Low breath into Chi while rolling
- Loose arms, loose neck and head
- Roll back up starting from coccyx vertebrae by vertebrae until your head is the last to come up

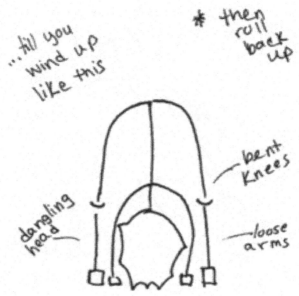

...till you wind up like this

* then roll back up

bent knees

dangling head

loose arms

Benefits

- Massages spine
- Releases tension

PANT LIKE A DOG

Practice

- Check for Long Spin, Soft Knees
- Feet under hips, or slightly outside
- Bend forward and put hands on knees
- Stick tongue out, resting on bottom teeth, and pant like a dog
- Bounce belly - wake up the Chi!
- Pant until mouth dries out and roll up. Repeat.

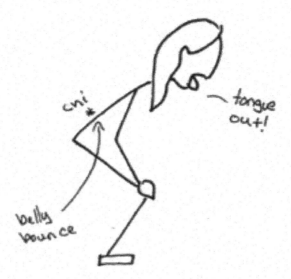

Benefits

- Low, energized breath
- Releases tension in throat

Questions

- Where does breath come from?
- Can you stick out your tongue farther?
- Is your belly bouncing?

VOICE

Now that the breath is low and supported, we can add sound without injuring our voice. When we have a free voice, we trust our voice to carry our stories. The next few exercises connect breath and body with voice in an easy and fun way.

SHAKE OUT SOUND - Play with high and low range of voice. Be silly with your voice.

Practice

- Individually shake right and left arm with sound
- Individually shake right and left leg with sound
- Shake an arm and a leg with sound, then switch
- Shake torso with sound
- Shake whole body with sound

  - Alternative: Individually shake out each limb while counting down from 10, then from 9, then 8, etc. Once the count is down to 0, shake entire body with sound.

SHIMMY DOWN ON A "HEY!"

Practice

- stretch arms up towards the sky on an inhale
- Swing your body! Start in head voice as your body shakes and rolls from the tips of your fingers to the floor and back up again.

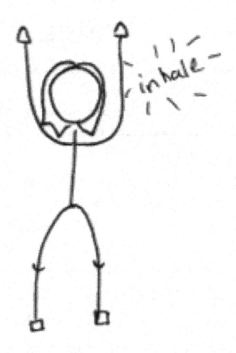

inhale

Shimmy &
Shake out "Hey"

MOTOR BOAT

Practice

Everyone pretends to hold a small motor boat in their hands and drive it by blowing raspberries (buzzing lips together). Explore range of voice as you drive the boat around the room. Drive a bigger boat, then an airplane.

Benefits

Warms up our lips, which help articulate our stories.

THROW "KA!" BALLS

Practice

- Make "K" sound on inhale and exhale (feel soft pallet stretch).
- Plant feet as if you were about to throw an object
- Hold the object or ball of energy in your hand and choose a far off target that is outside of the room.
- Inhale on "K" and wind up (like a baseball player)
- Exhale, full voice, when you throw the KA! ball at your target.
- Sound the whole time it takes your KA! ball to reach target
- End on SUPPORTED voice (don't let your voice get scratchy like KAAaaaa-a-a-a-a

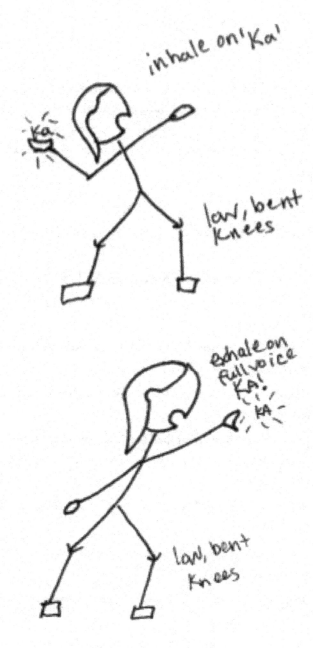

Benefits

- Stretches soft palette
- Makes room for sound
- Asks us to use imagination
- Asks us t commit to an OBJECTIVE
  - An objective is a goal. "I want my ball to reach the park."
  - Ask yourself: What do I want? You'll reach your objective with a full, supported voice and grounded body and breath.

CIRCLE EXERCISES & GAMES

PASS PULSE – The team passes a pulse around a circle while the leader of the game counts to see how fast it takes the pulse to go around the circle.

Practice

- Hold hands in a circle
- Leader starts pulse
- Counts one-one-thousand, two-one-thousand, etc., until the pulse reaches them again.
- Repeat 3x – 4x
- Try to beat each time.

Benefits

Sharpens focus, teamwork, and imagination.

Questions

What's an image that we can use to visualize the pulse as it goes around the circle? (a hose filled with water, a beam of light, etc.)

GESTURE PULSE

Practice

- Stand in Circle
- Leader makes strong gesture and sound, group repeats
- Next person makes gesture & sound, group repeats.
- Go around the circle
- Repeat 2x-3x.

Benefits

- Practice "don't think just do." (No time for pausing to think in this game, just follow your instincts.)
- Focus and physical listening skills
- builds relationships and trust when we repeat each other's gestures and sounds the exact way they made them.
- Practice dove-tailing: overlapping pulses to keep the energy moving from one person to the next.
- Use full body and voice to tell story.

Questions

- Why did that work well?
- Why didn't it work well?
- What makes it easier to correctly repeat gestures?

NAME GAME

Practice Start off in a circle. Like the pulse game, one person makes a gesture and sound, then the team repeats it. In the Name Game, each person makes a gesture and says their name in a way that describes the way they feel. After a new person goes, the cycle starts from the very beginning to help everyone learn the names of the group.

PASS "HA"

Practice Stand in a circle in ready position - Soft Knees, Long Spine!

Person A passes "HA" across circle to person B who passes "HA" to another person.

- Make Eye contact, take a step forward, and clap your hands at the person to whom your passing "HA"
- Keep the "HA" going around the circler without pauses.
- Everyone needs to think its their turn all the time to make sure "HA" is received without hesitation.

Benefits

- Direct eye contact, strong gestures and sounds demonstrate clear communication and confidence
- Clear communication demonstrates respect, support for the village and delivers clear stories

Alternative

The leader of the game can start passing abstract gestures and words around the circle clockwise and counterclockwise while "HA" is being passed.

- Passing "HA" and gestures at the same time is a fun challenge and will enhance village development—don't rush, stay focused and always stay in the game even when something goes awry

Benefits

- Builds focus and teamwork through strong gestures and sounds (simple stories)
- Village learns that they never abandon each other when their partner is busy with another task—keep sending the "HA" or the gesture!
- It's ALL about continuing the STORY!!!

Questions

- Why was that difficult or easy?
- How did you feel when you were in that exercise?
- What can we do to improve the passing of "HA" and gestures at the same time?

WHAT ARE YOU DOING?

Practice

Group stands in a circle. Person A steps into the middle of the circle and starts pantomiming a scene using strong gestures, sounds and/or words (i.e.: fishing in the sea). Person B jumps in and asks "Hey, what are you doing?" Person A says something completely different from their current action like "I'm plucking stars from the sky." Person B takes on the new action. Person A steps out of the circle leaving Person B to "pluck stars." Enter a new person to ask "Hey, what are you doing?" The cycle continues.

Benefits

- Allows full use of imagination

- Requires full use of body/voice to tell a short story
- Taking risks in front of each other makes for courageous story builders and sharers
- Trusting and practicing first impulses and 'gut' instincts

Questions & Comments

- How can you make the actions clearer?
- What would happen if you allowed stories to play out for few moments rather than immediately jumping in?

MACHINE

Practice

The group starts in a circle and votes on what type of machine they would like to make. It can be anything: A house machine, a cloud machine, a peace machine, etc.

Once the type of machine is chosen, one person steps into the centre and starts a movement and sound that represents the role they play in the machine. This is ABSTRACT we are not looking for realistic machinery (gears, levers, etc.)

After the first person starts the machine, each person in the circle adds to the machine.

Objective:

fill in the space at different heights, shapes, and actions. Each person in the machine has a role to play in the machine and fulfills that role using their movement and voice. Their role is their goal, which is their objective in the machine. An objective starts with "I want to _____"

- I want to build the roof
- I want to puff the clouds
- I want to stir the happiness

Questions/Comments

- Can you commit your full body and voice to your objective?
- Listen to each other. Can you create a stronger rhythm with your partners?
- Who do you depend on in the machine to do your job?
- Who depends on you?
- Ask the machine to speed up and slowdown in unison until it arrives at a full, organic stop.
- Were you leading? Following? Following the follower?

Benefits

- Responsibility to each other
- Dependability and trust

- Asks the group to focus on physically listening to each other.
- Teaches commitment and objectives.
- IMPORTANT: A machine doesn't work well, won't do its job unless all its parts are working well together...same with your Village.

Circle Time!

Activating the Village
AFP Circle Work: Videos

I realize these exercises may be difficult to imagine by yourself, so I asked some of my students to share them in action. This AFP Circle sequence is important to do in order, as listed here—the village will 'earn' each new step in complexity and difficulty. While you watch please stand up and DO, this is crucial—knowing is one thing, doing is quite another. As we have discussed multiple times in this book, this transition is crucial to the success of your story-building applications. The AFP Circle sequence videos can be viewed by scanning the code below.

1. **Establishing the Circle**

2. **Passing Electricity**

3. **HA-LLO Introduction**

4. **HA-LLO: Add Ons**

5. **Pass the Power**

6. **Pass the Power: Add Ons**

7. **Pass the Word**

8. **Voice and Movement Stories**

9. **Machines**

10. **Stacking Exercises and Lessons**

It is important to remember: These exercises should be considered **templates** for you, your students, your village, and your specific educational needs. The goal is *not* to make your students and village members Olympic level work passers, clappers and physical expressionists. The goals of are:

- To shift the impulses from the brain to the body

- To build a strong community, Village

- To provide an arena for *activating* the Village Rules

- To encourage expression and importance of personal and communal stories

- To create kinesthetic templates for the classroom to enhance learning. Once the village 'gets' the exercises their sounds and claps should be replaced by elements from the lesson plan, marrying their bodies and hearts to the content of the lesson. Bring the curriculum INTO the circle so the circle holds academic value and merit, not just the 'fun' place.

Activating the Village:
Specific Steps, Suggestions & Guidance

Always begin and end your village sessions together in the circle. One simple suggestion to your circle formations is the "democratic grasp.' There are two ways to hold the villager's hand next to you: *receiving*, palm out, or *giving*, palm down. Simple direction for your students: 'As you connect the circle into a village, one hand should *receive* the person next to you and the other should *give* to the person next to you. Accomplish this without using words or giving directions to each other.' We have done this simple task thousands of times. It's never as easy as it seems. You will find your students need to look to see what their hands are actually doing. It is worth mentioning that some of us are natural receivers and some of us are natural givers, which is why one may feel more natural than the other. This simple task is not only a nice way to prepare each villager to receive and give, but it also creates a powerful metaphor within the circle metaphor; the circle represents the unity of the village, and the hands represent the democracy that must exist within he village. Have fun connecting this metaphor to your needs: yin/yang, listen/speak, pause/go, happy/sad, external/internal, etc.

Beginning and ending each story-building session with the circle is an important pillar of AFP's work—we do it everywhere we go, with everyone we meet. We call it "Breathing In/Breathing Out," but you can call it whatever you like. It is individual and communal commitment to the village and the work that happens between the circles. It is a reaffirmation of the Village Rules and reminds us to leave everything not directly involved with our work outside. These distractions will be there after the village breathes out. The routine is simple:

1. Ask the village to join hands, making a circle. (call to order)

2. Ask the village to use the 'democratic grasp.' (We before Me)

3. Make sure the village is making a real circle not an uneven 'blob'. (Discipline)

4. Guide the village through three breaths together, as one.

   • Together, as a village, breathe in through your nose, out through your mouth.

   • As you inhale, breathe in all things you wish to bring to the village.

   • As you exhale, breathe out all things you wish to leave outside.

   • On the third breath, make a personal commitment to your growth (i.e., I want to use more of my body today)

   • Hold that commitment, wrap it in breath, and exhale.

   • *Commitments wrapped in breath cannot be reversed*

   • Allow the village to rest in silence after this third exhale. Eyes open, standing hand in hand, just being...

   • Allow this 'hanging out' after the third breath to increase in time as you progress through the process. The initial giggles and fidgeting will be replaced by a welcomed, powerful stillness. Students have referred to this time as 'getting right with themselves.'

5. After the third breath ask the students to give one word to describe how they feel. This description allows for the completion of the neural cycle and keeps the work from becoming precious or mystical. Words are tangible. All words are 'right.'

6. Above all, there should be an enhanced sense of presence after Breathing In/Out.

Once you have Breathed-In, you should move forward into your circle warm-up. After Breathing Out, the village is free to leave, return to the next part of their day, etc. This simple routine will become sacred to you and your students. This brief routine is directly related to meditation and mindfulness, two practices lauded for their multiple benefits. Contemplative educators include meditation in every lesson they teach as it is the path towards personal introspection. Without it, these educators profess, we are imposing the teacher's attitudes and ignoring the student's personal responses. Meditation does not require sitting in the lotus position on top of a sacred mountain in the Far East—this is a silly assumption. Meditation only requires the time and space to focus on the breath entering and exiting the body in the pursuit of the present moment. Mandating meditative time in your classes is, I believe, essential to positive student learning outcomes. Experiencing this mandate as part of your story-building process is a great opportunity to sample meditation and mindfulness in your classrooms.

Facilitating Circle Games—Village Lesson Vehicles

After the circle has been defined as a village expectation it will become your 'go to' stage for kinesthetic instruction. The nature of each game you play must have a direct connection to the lesson of the day. For instance, if authentic listening is the intended lesson, then the game(s) you play must all be, unapologetically, defined for that purpose. Your job as teacher is to publicly announce what successful and unsuccessful listening looks like during the games—you must catch your students in those 'teachable moments.' The circle is designed to be, above all else, an arena for teachable moments through active learning. Let's take a simple word passing game.

Game: Word Pass

Objectives: Enhance focus, listening, vocal clarity and presence.

Instructions:

In the circle, ask each student to drop their hands to their sides. Explain that there are three positions for their heads/eyes to focus. Position 1: Straight ahead, eye focus 10 degrees above the head of the person across from you. Position 2: Head turns to look at the person directly to your right. Position 3: Head turns to look at the person directly to your left. Explain that positions 2 and 3 are used when you pass a word to the person next to you and the goal is to always return to position 1 after passing a word to the left or right—do not follow the word around the circle, always return to position 1, this is your powerful place of presence and readiness. When moving between positions 1, 2 and 3 do so with machine like precision and speed. Never linger or drift between positions, always move swiftly and cleanly—take pride in your physical clarity. Now let's add words to the movements. Starting at position 1, the teacher will turn to position 2 and share a word with the person to their right and then return to position 1. Everyone in the circle should be at position 1 unless they are sharing a word apposition 2 or 3, then immediately returning to position 1. The person to the teacher's right receives the word and shares it with the person next to them at position 2, and then (you guessed it) returns immediately to position 1, their place of readiness. The word should be passed in full volume (no whispering) with clarity and precision. The goal is to pass the same word, unchanged, around the entirety of the circle. Once a word has been passed successfully around the circle the teacher can ask some important questions:

"What made that work well?"

"What happened when the word changed?"

"What happened when the word stopped?"

"What do you need to do individually to ensure the word moves successfully?"

"What do you need to do as a village to guarantee success in this game?"

"What can we do as a village to impede this game's success?"

Now, let's pass a word the other direction. Ask the students to focus, be present, always return to position 1 and remember the primary goal of the game—this goal is a direct activation of many village rules including *We Agree That Story is First*. The story is the single word making it around the circle unfettered. If the village cannot successfully tell this simple story together, it will be impossible to tell larger, more layered, complex stories later. Thus, we are never playing these circle games to become great circle game players. We are playing these games to activate and experience the simple building blocks of story building. If I was a long-distance track coach I would never ask my runners to run a marathon at the first practice. I would begin with stretching and a short running distance of ¼ mile. This ¼ mile is a building block, a part of the eventual marathon that requires attention and precision before moving on to longer distances. So too is the word pass game—we increase the number of words moving around the circle as we realize the importance of each individual word making it around the circle. The 'marathon' of the word game will be multiple words moving around the circle simultaneously in both directions without losing any of the words—whew!

So, returning to the game, we have now passed one word completely around the circle to the right and one word around the circle to the left (clockwise and counterclockwise). Next, the teacher (the words always begin with one person—eventually, the word maker can be assigned to a student. This is an excellent reward for students who may not excel in traditional academics but do stand out in kinesthetic education) passes 2 words, one in each direction, around the circle. The students know everything they need to know for story success here: stay focused on the story, always return to position 1 after passing, speak clearly and loudly, stay present. As the village improves with this game the teacher can add more words. The village will eventually be able to maintain an unlimited number of words simultaneously. They will build their abilities to eventually run the 'marathon' of word pass. This and other similar circle games are excellent measurement tools for the village's togetherness—the more complete the village, the more complex the challenges of the circle games. You will note a tangible sense of village confidence and pride as they develop their story building skills.

While the teacher's intended lesson focus may have been enhanced authentic listening, you will note that the teaching opportunities are seemingly endless with this and other circle games. The most important factor is for the teacher to catch the students in the active moment and use that moment to physically illustrate a lesson. Don't be shy and never assume you are ruining the flow of the game by stopping it to make a point—quite honestly, the entire reason for the game is to provide experiential opportunities to teach and learn. In the end, who cares about how many words were passed? Every action is merely a lesson vehicle. Every lesson is a small atom of the story building process. Multiple lessons combined create the matter and stuff of stories. Never allow the games to move forward without reminding the village they are acquiring the skills to improve the world—to tell their stories.

We will share multiple AFP circle games throughout this book. Please, please, please adapt these games to best fit the needs of your students, schools and organizations. Create new games that evolve out of our games. The 'what' of the games are far less important than the 'why' of the games.

Always, always, always build the lesson bridges from the games to the story building to the lives of your students.

Bringing Individual Gifts to the Village

As you and your students become increasingly comfortable with the routines of the village you will note an important product: You are all getting to know each other in important, meaningful and substantive ways. As the village develops and its rules dictate behavior naturally, preconceived assumptions will dissolve. The hard, bold lines of social cliques will surrender to the oneness of the circle. Negative nicknames for students that may be popular outside of class are no longer used or acceptable in the village. How did this peaceful world happen? Magic? Fear? By chance? Absolutely not—you have been building the village step-by-step, expectation by expectation, action by action, story by story.

As the work in the circle becomes more advanced you will see more vulnerability from your students. When mammals are comfortable and trusting of their environments, they share more of themselves—they will embrace risk and try new things. They will share more of their stories. This is an excellent opportunity for a new assignment for your students:

1. What special talent or unique skill do you have as an individual?

   - This should be something most people do not know about you.

   - It can be anything you consider special.

   - It must be shared physically

   - Examples: tap dancing, beat-boxing, martial arts, knuckle popping, bubble blowing, musical instrument playing, burping loudly, etc.

2. Bring your "gift" to share with the village next class meeting.

   This gift sharing should happen in the circle, while standing and the sharer simply goes to the middle of the circle to offer their gift to the village—sacred space. This simple exercise will provide opportunities for students to showcase their specialness without bragging or showing off. This is also an opportunity to get to know each other on a deeper level. You may never know one of your students was a Tai Chi master or played the clarinet or could throw darts with such precision! There will be students who will share silly gifts (drinking two liters of soda in one gulp)— this is completely fine, expected and recommended. You do not want this to turn into American Idol or some other ridiculous competition. This is simply another page you are offering your students to add to their stories. My experience with this assignment suggests some guaranteed results:

   - You will get to know your students in new ways (personally and culturally).

   - Your students will get to know each other in new ways.

   - Perspectives about each other will change.

- You will further unite the village with shared vulnerabilities.

- You will stock your village library with unique possibilities for your story to be used later (See **Act IV: Sharing Your Story**)

Examples of Village Rules from Local Schools

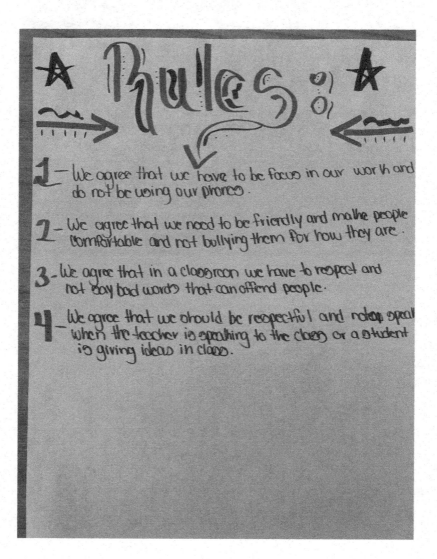

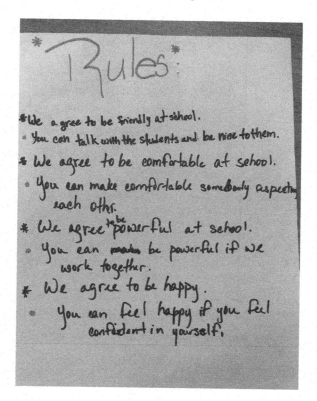

Rules:

*We agree to be friendly at school.
- You can talk with the students and be nice to them.
* We agree to be comfortable at school.
- You can make comfortable somebody aspecting each other.
* We agree to be powerful at school.
- You can be powerful if we work together.
* We agree to be happy.
- You can feel happy if you feel confident in yourself.

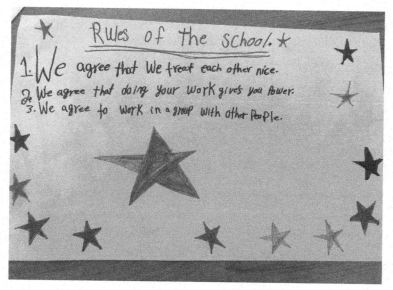

Rules of the school.
1. We agree that we treat each other nice.
2. We agree that doing your work gives you power.
3. We agree to work in a group with other people.

"There is no greater agony
than bearing an untold story inside you."

Maya Angelou

The Story Building Process
Act II: Surfacing the Story

Remember, there is no set amount of time for the creation of the village. You will be spending entire class sessions only working on the village rules, warm-up exercises and community games. This time allowance is not only expected, but also mandatory. There is no bell that will ring when the group has united and become a village. You will know when the village rules are complete when there is consensus amongst the village after ample time to discuss, debate and wordsmith. You will know when the circle games are truly the warm-up preparation of the meeting and not the entirety of your time together when your students, quite literally, ARE the village rules. There will be a day during these early stages where the students will physically and emotionally own the exercises and games. What was once clumsy and awkward will become athletic and smooth. The sound of embarrassed giggles will be replaced by committed shouts. The amoeba of a circle, loose and amorphous, will be a defined radius, with equal distance between each person. Selfless sharing and courageous collaborations will replace the stifled impulses and insecurities. This all sounds wonderful, doesn't it? It may not surprise you that I believe this is how every classroom should begin and end its work each and every day. Hey, a guy can dream, right? If I had a magic potion that you could spray on all your students to make the village happen instantly, I would give it to you. I don't have this. In the meantime, while we are awaiting this mysterious elixir, the only magic I can offer you is, *time*. You must take time to allow the village to define itself. This is not work to be rushed through to get to the story stuff—this is the stuff that stories are built on. No village, no foundation. No foundation, no building. To appease the teacher-timer-clock-watchers out there, here's a practical goal: Eventually, the circle preparations should take 10 minutes to complete.

Theme = the '*What*' of the Story

Now that the village is sweaty, smiling and present we are ready for the next step of the story building process. The Village has been created so you know *Who* will be doing the work. It's now time to create the *What* of your story, the **Theme**. The term 'theme' gets thrown around a lot without much regard for consistency. Single words (i.e. Revenge) are not themes, they're words. A theme, in AFP land, is the central lesson, moral or message that drives the story. It's what the protagonist(s) learn after the completion of their journey(s) when they have the opportunity to answer the major dramatic question of the story. Stories are lesson vehicles, just mechanisms for delivering important messages. A theme must be a concise, defined, brief phrase that can economically encompass the entire point of a story. It is most effective to think of a story's theme as a "bumper sticker," short, concise and quickly communicative. 'Revenge' is not a theme; 'Revenge is the Root of Evil' is a theme. 'Pride' is not a theme; 'Pride can be your enemy' is a theme. "Connect' is not a theme; 'You can always connect to someone' is a theme. You can ruin every Disney story for a new viewer by whispering in their ear before the movie begins, 'The answer is in her/his heart." I don't mock Disney here, how can I argue with their storytelling success?! I humbly bow to their military commitment to *theme*. Another effective way to assist your students is to imagine their theme ideas must fit on a t-shirt. Both bumper stickers and t-shirts share the need to communicate ideas quickly, in a glance as someone walks or drives past. This clean phrase is our eventual product.

These are simple ideas, not easy to accomplish. Here's the process for surfacing what your story is about by creating the **Theme**.

Theory-to-Action: Prompting the Theme: Text, Images and Current Events

You can't just explain what a theme is and expect your students to produce quality examples. The village needs parameters and guidelines or they will be dipping into the pool of everything to find their themes—too much freedom. You must narrow the focus of choices by providing a theme *prompt*. This is an important tool for you to consider as you begin your process. This is your opportunity to steer the process towards your learning objectives. A favorite director of mine once put it like this, "I don't direct plays, I just open and close doors for actors. I close far more than I open." Remember, story building is not a Democracy—you are in charge. What do you want to accomplish? What are the learning objectives for the particular unit you are presently working on? What issues do you hope to address outside of the traditional curriculum? These are all important questions to answer before you begin to help your students surface the theme of their story. The *prompt* is a tool to encourage an open discussion about a particular topic. The *prompt* can be a short video, song, poem, image or photo. This *prompt* should be chosen carefully. It is best to keep the *prompt* short and impactful; a quotation will serve the village more effectively than a lengthy essay and a stanza from a poem will serve the village more effectively than the entire poem. I have found provocative photos to work extremely well.

Let me offer three examples.

Example #1: Poetry

Imagine a teacher who is interested in her students making personal connections to the ideas of 'freedom' and 'slavery.' She uses as her prompt these two stanzas from Maya Angelou's *I Know Why the Caged Bird Sings*

> *The free bird thinks of another breeze and the trade winds soft through the sighing trees and the fat worms waiting on a dawn-bright lawn and he names the sky his own. But a caged bird stands on the grave of dreams his shadow shouts on a nightmare scream his wings are clipped and his feet are tied so he opens his throat to sing*

Project the prompt on a shared screen in the room. If a screen (projector, smartboard, etc.) is unavailable write on white board or chalkboard.

1. Remind the village of the lesson you are working on in class.

2. Ask the village to read the poem independently three times.

3. Ask volunteers to read it aloud.

4. Ask if there are any 'sense' questions; make sure everyone understands the poem.

5. Clear a white board, chalkboard, or large pad of paper in plain view of the village. Don't erase poem.

6. Ask the villagers to share **single words** that this poem surfaces/evokes in them. How does this poem make them **feel**?

#Breadcrumb Alert#

Hearstorming.

Too often, brain-storming is confused with experiential learning. I disagree. In my experience, brain-storming is the audible version of thinking. What we hear are the answers to the test in the air instead of scribbles on a scantron sheet. The ideas are heard but restricted to the brain. When we are building stories, we are more concerned with feelings than thoughts. Feelings will engage the village in shared, visceral, physical experiences—these experiences will produce meaningful stories to share. When we open the creative process to the village, we are hoping to surface ideas that make us feel something worth sharing. Feelings come from the heart, not the brain. Students need to rehearse assigning words to their feelings. Students need to know that what they feel matters. Feelings are physical experiences where the central nervous system completes a full cycle from impulse to body to language. If we just think out loud, we cut that cycle short, thus never completely communicating our personal experiences. These personal experience cycles happen in quick bursts during the heart storming process. They happen instinctively, impulsively, and organically without filters. Theses personal experiences remind your students that they matter. Heart storming can be liberating for the village and is something we return to often during the story building process.

7. Write down every word they share. There are no 'right' or 'wrong' words. Be particular about how they wish to spell, capitalize, hyphenate, etc. Handle their words with care.

8. Remind the village: If a word has meaning to you, it matters.

9. Allow for discussions and debates.

10. 1The more words the better—the board should be packed and messy. Those words are their mini stories: unrestricted impulse responses using language.

Example #2: Photo

Here's a photo prompt to ignite heart-storming for the same learning objective (Freedom and Slavery):

1. Remind the village of the lesson you are working on in class.

2. Ask the village to view the photo quietly.

3. Ask volunteers to share what they see.

4. Ask if there are any questions; make sure everyone understands there are many ways to view something.

5. Clear a white board, chalkboard, large pads of paper in plain view of the village. Don't hide photo.

6. Ask the villagers to share **single words** that this poem evokes in them.—NO THINKING! What do their hearts say? How does the photo make them **feel**?

7. Write down every word they share. There are no right or wrong words. Be particular about how they wish to spell, capitalize, hyphenate, etc. Handle their words with care.

8. Remind the village: if a word has meaning to them, it matters.

9. Allow for discussions and debates.

10. The more words the better—the board should be packed and messy. Those words are their mini stories: unrestricted impulse responses using language

Example #3: Current Event

Current events are excellent prompt tools. I am mystified when teachers ignore important current events in the classroom. To be fair, it is a tricky task to weave the bombing of Paris into the fabric of the tailored lesson plan. Teachers spend a great deal of time and energy preparing lesson plans—I understand the need to stick to the schedule.

Additionally, very few university education programs teach this type of improvisational dexterity. I think it's crucial. Including current events in the classroom falls into the category of engaging students in 'difficult conversations.' Starting the conversation tends to be the most difficult part. Using a current event as your story prompt (even if it's the story of one day) is a structured way to jump into a potentially loaded topic while connecting the content to what you are working on in class.

Inmate Died After Going 7 Days Without Water

May 1, 2017

(CNN) Before Terrill Thomas died from dehydration in a Milwaukee County Jail cell, inmates say they heard him repeatedly beg jail guards for water, an investigator said during an inquest into Thomas' death.

Inmate Marcus Berry said that "starting on Monday and every day after that, Thomas asked every (correctional officer) for water because the water in his cell was shut off," testified Detective Kyle Mrozinski of the Milwaukee Police Department, which is investigating the 38-year-old's death.

1. Remind the village of the unit you are working on in class.

2. Ask the village to read the story quietly to themselves.

3. Ask volunteers to read story aloud.

4. Ask if there are any questions; make sure everyone understands the context of the event.

5. Post the prompt on a white board, chalkboard, large pad of paper in plain view of the village. Don't hide the current event.

6. Ask the villagers to share **single words** that this current event evokes in them. NO THINKING! What do their hearts say? How does the event make them **feel**?

7. Write down every word they share. There are no right or wrong words. Be particular about how they wish to spell,

capitalize, hyphenate, etc. Follow their lead, handle their words with care.

8. Remind the village: if a word has meaning to then, it matters.

9. Allow for discussions and debates.

10. The more words the better—the board should be packed and messy. Those words are their mini stories: unrestricted impulse responses using language.

11. Read all of the words aloud as a village.

12. Now that they've heard the words, any additions?

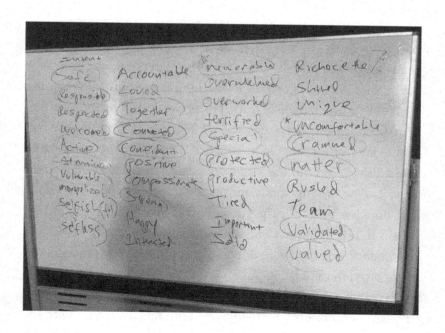

Heartstorming Process Board

Theory-to-Action:
Respectfully Omitting & Identifying the Greatest Hits

As you look at the sloppy, wonderful word mess the village has created on the board remind them that this is their story as it stands in the process now. Its not ready for an audience yet, which is why its messy, abstract and nonsensical...just a bunch of words inspired by a prompt. Ask the village to look over their words and make observations. What do they see? How do they feel? What connections can be made? Are their consistencies that occurred organically? Once this discussion has happened (guided by Village Rules and Heart Storming principles), remind the village that all of these words are worthwhile and important, but an important part of creating stories is that we must squeeze the essence from the whole event so that it can move through the magic and come out, Story. We cannot share everything we experience together with our future audience. Anne Frank was in hiding for over two years, but we can only keep the audience in the theater for two hours. We must, as a village, practice the delicate art of omitting and editing. Remind the village of their first rule: *We agree that Story is First.* We must put our personal feelings, our egos, aside and do what's best for the story. This is an obviously important lesson to teach our students on multiple levels. They know and have heard this before undoubtedly, but have they practiced it? More often than not, the answer is no...unless you have athletes in the village who have played on successful sport teams. They are experienced 'story first' villagers with much to share with the rest of the village. Ask them to share their 'team first' experiences. This is a nice opportunity to include the jocks who may feel disconnected from the artistic process thus far. The village NEEDS the jocks—they are important! Here are the steps to respectfully identifying the 'greatest hits' theme words:

1. Conclude the messy word board observations discussion.

2. Remind them of the prompt.

3. Ask the village to look over the words and select those only that resonate most intensely with them individually; the words that make them **feel** the most.

4. Remind them that omitting certain words doesn't mean they 'don't like them' or that they are 'bad words.' In fact, those words made the 'greatest hits' possible.

5. Omit synonyms. Allow the village to discuss and debate which word in groups of similar words to keep. Allow for nuanced differences expressed by villagers to justify keeping both words up.

6. Encourage economy—narrow the total number of 'greatest hits' down as much as possible without losing important ideas.

7. When the village has its 'greatest hits' words, erase the words that are no longer needed. Emphasize you are doing this for clarity not judgment.

8. Ask the village is they see any trends, patterns, relationships with the remaining words. Ask if they'd like you to move the words so they visually reflect those trends, patterns or relationships.

9. Place the words as the village demands. *They are making sense of the word list, bringing order to the chaos, trying to create meaning, attempting to format a story.*

10. Read the 'greatest hits' theme words aloud as a village.

11. Now that they've heard the words, any final additions? Omissions?

Theory-to-Action:
Breaking the Village into Collaborative Groups

#Breadcrumb Alert#

There will be multiple times in the story building process where the village is separated into smaller groups, given a specific collaborative assignment and asked to return to the whole village to share what they have created together. These break out collaborations always have a time limit. The village sends small hunting parties out into the wild with an expectation they will return with gifts for the village. This separating, moving out in smaller pieces and returning to the whole demonstrates an important, intentional rhythm to story building. Clasp your hands together. Now, separate your hands and spread your fingers out wide as you move your hands away from each other. Bring your hands back together in the original clasp. Repeat this action several times. What does this rhythm remind you of? (Hint: Something your body does naturally thousands of times each day and it rhymes with Preathing) **Breathing,** *you are correct! Story building is a natural human process like breathing. We ensure this important point by duplicating the breathing rhythm within the story building process.*

Keeping the greatest hits in clear view, separate the village into three smaller groups. This is a good opportunity to be strategic about who you choose for each group—do you need to separate friends? Would it be unfair to place all the shy students in one group? Can you place a natural leader in each group without it being obvious? Be mindful of these decisions—everything matters and each teacher-choice you make during the process, large or small, will find its way into your story.

Theme group assignment:

1. Introduce yourselves to each other using circle Name Game-Stay Physical (2-3 minutes)

2. Look at the theme greatest hits board as a group—discuss responses with each other. What are those words trying to say? Listen to each other—practice village rules.

3. Use the greatest hits words to inspire the creation of three possible themes. Remember, themes are 'bumper stickers.' The themes don't need to contain all or any of the words on the board—they must be inspired by the words on the board.

4. It is best to consider the wording of your theme possibilities out loud for each other. Don't be precious with them, let them rip, the more you have to choose from the better!

5. Discuss the ideas with each other out loud in your groups. It's OK to disagree, but always offer potential solutions when you do.

6. One group member will write them down—one group member will report the three themes to the village when we return to each other. (10 minutes).

#Breadcrumb Alert#

The small group collaborations are actually applied research modules. You must always come to listen and observe. Never underestimate the value of your physical presence amongst your students. You visiting the collaborative groups will convey to your students that their work is valued, that you care about them and that they are empowered to create without you. That means you must not contribute or 'fix' their work! It is difficult for us to allow our students to make mistakes— but they will never learn anything if we continuously fix their work. Allow these group collaborations to be messy and loud. You are there to keep them on track, remind them of the assignment, remind them of the village rules and keep time. You are not mute during your group visits—you can certainly speak, but do so only in the name of assisting the group's completion of the assignment. Some groups will claim they are 'stuck,' and therefore unable to produce the product in the assigned time. During these instances (and the will happen) inform the group that the assignment is not optional, and they are bound by the village rules. Then, proceed with the most important thing a teacher can do: Ask questions! What do you feel when you hear those words? What do they say about slavery and freedom? What do YOU want to say about these issues? What lesson do you wish the world to learn about these issues? Fill in the blank: The world will be a better place if _____? If you drove a freedom/slavery car, what would the bumper sticker say? Encourage each group to complete the assignment on time. Remind them this is not a competition—what their group creates is the result of their healthy collaboration—A+! It's not about them (me), it's about the village (we) and the Story. If there are reoccurring issues as you move through the groups, feel free to freeze the room and collectively clarify, then unfreeze the room and ask them to return to their group work.

#Breadcrumb Alert#

*The more freedom and safety the village creates, the louder the collaborative group work sessions will be. We always warn teachers and staff at the schools we visit that its going to get loud during the workshop. While we realize we have all been taught that loud is rude and silence is polite, AFP believes that loud is a great sign of freedom during the collaborative process; during their applied research. We never support disrespectfully speaking out during inappropriate times—we make that distinction clear and so should you. This allowing for noise is important for AFP, as we cannot say "Your story matters" one moment, but "Shut up" in the next moment. Two strategies to offer: First, **specifically clarify** when students can be noisy and when they can't before the group work begins. Be firm and clear and remind them this is the discipline mandated by the village rules. Beyond the thin mask of their complaints, students love structure and rules. Second, as the noise level increases, your teacher voice will lose its power—your students simply won't be able to hear you and you will damage your vocal instrument trying. We have found repeated clapping patterns to work well in these situations. You clap a pattern; they repeat until you have their full attention. This may seem like summer camp, but that's fine, summer camp lessons are worth resurfacing. Clapping is primal, rhythmic, and precise. The students will enjoy it and soon recognize it as the collective call to order. Don't stop the clapping until you have the bodies and eyes of each villager before you.*

Special Note: Discipline and Tough Love

Your students will quickly embrace the freedom and ethos of the village. This can be misinterpreted as a free for all and that its ok to say whatever you want *whenever you want (Woodstock revisited). This could not be further from the truth. 'There can be no freedom without discipline' remember? You must provide clear, defined structure as you police the village rules until they become learned habits of your students. They will attempt to push the limits whenever possible—you must draw those lines with authority. Good teaching is like good parenting: Our job is not to get our students to like us, our job is to get our students to love themselves.*

Discipline and Structure are acts of Love.

7. Announce to the village when they have 5 minutes (halftime) remaining in their collaborative groups. Continue to wander, listen, and visit groups.

8. Announce to the village when they have 2 minutes remaining in their collaborative groups.

9. Announce to the village to make final choices and choose who will report their collaborative group's work to the village.

10. Clap the village back together.

You will learn a great deal about the village and your individual students during these collaborative breakout sessions. Who are your leaders? Who are your followers? Who are your worriers? Who are your clowns? Who are your pleasers? Who are our rebels? Who are your model collaborators? There are many more archetypical roles that will be assumed and defined—it happens every process, just like it happens in every class you teach or group you manage. One thing you will learn for certain is that each village (and individual villager) will treat *time* differently. How you manage time throughout the process is crucial. Again, since so much of what we do can be fun and free, we must capitalize on every opportunity to illustrate the discipline necessary to create meaningful stories. Time is a valuable tool to define discipline. Being on time every time is the activation of a village rule: *We agree to respect each other as collaborators and as people.* It is a sign of respect for the village, the process and the story to be on time, every time.

Students will respond in a variety of ways when confronted with strict time requirements. My experience suggests that students come to the village with a wide variety of concepts (putting it mildly) about time. These concepts come from their homes of course, but also, and perhaps more importantly here, they come from their former teachers. Some teachers are very relaxed about deadlines and others are quite strict. Some teachers follow through on timeliness rules and consequences while others do not. I have found that most students do not see time as a vehicle for respect and will do just about anything to justify their habitual tendencies to being at odds with strict time concerns. It's not their fault—their former teachers have not done their jobs. I have found that *publicly* adhering to time rules and expecting 100% compliance from the village works well. By *publicly*, I mean to announce, in the presence and earshot of the village, how consistent lateness issues are being handled as they happen. This is not an intention to humiliate the student who is breaking the time rules. Rather, it is an affirmation to those who are abiding by the rules (always the majority), confirming to them that you are doing your job by policing the village rules, thus supporting and protecting the village. This may take a few repetitions, but when the late student is reminded that this is a village rule and they will be asked to leave the village if they cannot practice the rules, then time becomes important. The offending student will undoubtedly feel attacked and the rest of the village sympathetic—this is normal. Explain to the offending student, simply and directly:

- This is a village rule and everyone in the village is expected to comply 100%.

- It's not about 'you,' it's about the village.

- If I didn't care about you and your future, I would let it go and say nothing. I care about you, so I'm going to be tough on you.

- Ask the student: 'What will you do to repair the negative impact your lateness had on the village?'

Part of the uncomfortable reactions you will receive from this direct, public methodology stems from the fact that it contrasts with most western education classroom management styles. Typically, teachers spend an imbalanced amount of precious class time on the disruptive students, leaving most of the rule-following students on their own to 'read quietly.' Let me repeat this reality: In a class of 30 students, we tend to focus precious instruction time on 1 student while ignoring the educational needs of 29 students. This model eliminates most of the students from the life lesson at hand. We must embrace this teaching opportunity by making the lesson public, thus including the **entire village** in an important life lesson of responsibility, respect, collaboration, and cause-and-effect. Those lessons are assumed unless made active through public clarity and inclusion. Your late students will eventually become timely, and your time-abiding students comforted and rewarded— both groups will be thankful you took the more difficult road to saying something—silence is easy poison. We call this *modeling* behavior for your students; definitely not easy, definitely the best choice for the village.

#Breadcrumb Alert#

Gacaca

Amongst the many lessons we have learned in Rwanda, their homegrown, precolonial judicial system, Gacaca (ga-CHA-cha), resurfaces the most often. Loosely translated as "Justice on the grass," this community method of conflict resolution helped bring over 1,000,000 perpetrators to justice efficiently and effectively. Based on the pillars of promoting forgiveness by victims, ownership of guilt by criminals, and reconciliation in communities as a way to move forward, Gacaca helped Rwandans to rewrite their post-genocide narrative. These same goals have assisted our story-building communities overcome internal obstacles so their stories can continue being built. While the severity and horrifically high stakes of genocide are not what you will confront as you build stories, the foundational aspect of public apology, public forgiveness, and community-defined reparations, will provide extremely valuable, active lessons for your students, their stories and their lives.

A **Gacaca** proceeding in post-1994 Rwanda

When encountering time restraints and deadlines, some students will simply panic if the work is not near completion in their group at the two-minute warning —their fear of failure will paralyze them, and they will convince themselves of pending doom and gloom. In acting terms, these students are playing their *obstacle*. We know that if you play anything other than an *action* your acting will be ineffective. This is true here too. When we announce the two-minute warning during group collaborations, we always look for those students/groups in panic states. They may be fearing failure, or they may really need more time to complete the task. Regardless of the reason, when you notice a time concern, clap the village together and ask them, as a village, if they'd like to have additional time to complete the task. Usually, there is (at least) one group that will react as though they have just won the lottery—they will vote for more time. If one group needs more time, that is enough to justify sending the entire village (all groups) back to work for an additional 5 minutes. I always like to confirm these decisions by saying 'The village has spoken." Several lessons were taught here: the village realizes they have ownership of the process, they realize there will be moments when they make choices without the teacher, they understand the importance of time in the process, and you have confirmation that they care about the work…why else would they ask for more time? There is a flipside of course—what about the groups who finish early? These will be easy to identify during your collaborative group visits as the students in these 'finished' groups will all be staring at their cellphones. I put 'finished' in quotes because there is no such thing as 'finished' in the story building process. Time is an opportunity to get closer to perfection—something I've never seen before. This sprinting-to-be-finished is also the result of their past family and educational experiences. Many of our brightest, most school-ready students have been fed the false notion that product is more important process, so those who finish first win. I am a bit embarrassed to say that this is a very American idea. I always ask my early birds, "What are you all doing on your cellphones?" "We're finished!" they say expecting a trophy. "Let me hear your perfect themes then." One of the students unfolds a paper from their pocket and reads me three themes. This is your opportunity to ask questions...lots of questions, until they realize they must return to their collaborative work to refine and expand what they have come up with. Can they create more than three themes? Play the devils' advocate, "Are those themes reflective of the whole group or just one person?" "Is it in the best interest of the village for other groups to be seeing you disengaged from the process?" "What is the lesson to be learned?" "How do these themes reflect the prompt, and can they be extended to universal themes?" "Where else in life would these themes be relevant?" "Would you change the language in different contexts?" And so on...you get the idea, there are reasons to ask for more time and never reasons to be done early. We will pick up the process from where we left off...

11. Ask the village how the collaborative process went for them. Which village rules were applied, which ignored? Ask them to finish this sentence, "That collaborative process worked best when we _____." Saying these ideas aloud is important as it moves the *knowing* to *doing*.

12. Ask each group to present their themes to the village. They have already chosen one person from their group to report their work.

13. Write down each group's three themes on the board. Ask the rest of the village to respond to each group's themes. Village Rules apply during feedback sessions. It is best to frame these discussions by asking "What was clear or unclear?" vs. "What was good or bad." The goal is not to

have one group's work liked more than others, the goals is to collect the best possible themes for our story: *We agree that Story is first.*

14. Once all themes are up on the board, ask the village to look at the prompt they first viewed, the words they started with, greatest hits words and now the collection of themes. This is an evolution they can see and be proud of—its hard work.

15. Refocus on just the themes and ask the village to make observations regarding repetition, patterns, language, and sequences. What do they **feel**?

16. 16. Send the same groups back to a new collaborative session. Assignment: Choose your group's favorite theme of the three and physically communicate this theme for the village (10 minutes.) Reminders: the games during the circle warm-up, use each other as parts to the whole, use sounds but not words and abstract movement is more communicative than literal movement...it should be noisy!

We use and depend on *abstract* movement and sounds as important creative tools throughout the process. *Abstract* can be defined as: 'Existing in thought or as an idea but not having a concrete existence.' In our work, we take the idea to the level of *Abstract Expressionism* that can be defined as:

AFP Students using **Abstract Movement** to tell their story

'The outward expression of inward idea using the actor's entire instrument.' *Abstract Expressionism* allows for an economy of communication that is both extremely personal and universal at the same time. The abstraction of body and voice allows for a fullness of expression without getting lost in the literal person trying to literally be or feel something. Literal communication is emphasized in the movies, television, and social media we consume. *Abstract* is emphasized in child's play, dance, and our dreams. Literal is filled with limitations; abstract has no boundaries. Example: If I ask you to *literally* illustrate the word 'Pizza' you might pantomime eating a slice of pizza or making an entire pizza, both as people doing the actions we are familiar with. This will work well for charades, not for story building. If I ask you to *abstractly* illustrate the word pizza, I would stress the importance of how pizza makes you **feel** and then to use your whole body and voice to illustrate that/those feeling(s). This expression will change based on how you feel about pizza. If you love pizza the expression will look very different from someone who despises pizza. *Abstraction* will also provide more freedom for your students than literal portrayals. It will be daunting for your students to literally be a 'person in love' in front of the village—that's adolescent kryptonite! It will be far less inhibitive for your students to *abstractly* communicate the 'idea or feeling of love'—they have an entire library of contemporary music icons to pull from. When students first attempt *abstract* movement, they typically resort to their dance moves and look at me apologetically until I tell them, that's it, exactly! *Abstract expressions* should look more like dance than duplications of people in reality. *One Word Abstractions* is an excellent game to inform and activate the use of Abstract vs. Literal.

Local Teachers experience 1-Word Abstract Stories

*Important Note: It is always a good idea to follow your verbal introduction of new concepts with an exercise or game to complete the learning process physically, *Theory-to-Action*. Exercises should also be used when the village is confused or unclear about a particular idea or concept. The exercises throughout this book and the AFP Story Building process should be added to your teaching library and utilized when you feel the need to clarify, illuminate and define lessons for your students. Once you personally learn these exercises, you own them and they are yours to use at your discretion. As a rule, it is better to use more physicality than less—be liberal with your activation, it will never damage the lesson, the students will love it and you will undoubtedly learn something you never thought of. The worst-case scenario: You and your students will have fun. Can you think of a better worst-case scenario?!

AFP student-artists demonstrate 1-Word Abstract Stories, Buffalo Public Schools

Picking up...

17. After the groups have had sufficient time, clap them back to the village.

18. Ask the village how this collaborative process went for them. Which village rules were applied, which ignored? Ask them to finish this sentence, "That collaborative

process worked best when we _____." Saying these ideas aloud is important as it moves the *knowing* to *doing*.

19. Remind them of the importance of moving the work from the brain to the body to the heart.

20. Remind them of the breathing rhythm emulated in the collaborative village process.

21. Ask which group would like to share first. Each group shares their physical theme with the village and says the theme only after they have abstractly expressed it.

22. Ask the rest of the village to respond to each group's theme. Village Rules apply during feedback sessions.

23. After all of the groups have shared and received village feedback, refocus on just the themes and ask the village to make observations regarding repetition, patterns, language and sequences. What do they feel?

24. Keep each group's theme they just shared on the board and remove the two themes each group did not use in their performances.

25. As a village, heart storm until **one theme** surfaces from those remaining on the board. It can be a combination of themes left or words borrowed from one to plug into another. This will be the **theme** of your story.

26. Keep the heart storming theme boards: words, greatest hits, multiple themes, etc. These will be helpful to refer to throughout the process. Take photos of the boards. * It is a good idea to create an e-library for the process. This will be an important place to share and coordinate information, especially between class meetings. Give access to the entire village for appropriate folders.

27. Remind the village: Every time we build stories, we build many stories on our way to the one we will share this time. We are never throwing ideas away like garbage—we are recognizing that every idea was an important step towards our eventual central theme. We never would have come to our chosen theme without the words and themes we omitted—these ideas, performances, exercises, discussions, debates, compromises, responses and questions all created our theme. *The village has spoken.*

Surfacing Theme Through 'My Story'

Another strategy that may be used to prompt the theme is using the *My Story* assignment, which are basically the personal stories of your students as a reflection tool. These may be used in conjunction with the above prompts or independently. *My Story* tends to work best after the village has been exposed to a powerful and high-staked shared experience. These experiences can be intentional (international travel, community organization visit, guest speaker) or unintentional (local event, community concern, national disaster). I use *My Story* with my villages upon our return from Rwanda and other international experiences. *My Story* also involves a homework component that may be attractive to your coursework. Here's the *My Story* outline for prompting your village's story theme:

1. Identify the high-staked event that will prompt the prompt. Let's use the shared experience of a Holocaust survivor who came and spoke with the village about her experiences in a concentration camp. Dense, difficult, emotional material.

2. Define the **objectives, structure** and **clarity** of the assignment: "Based on your personal experience from our recent

guest speaker, you will be asked to create a *Personal Story* based on that experience."

3. The **objective** is for you to share how this experience made you feel and what lesson(s) you feel would be important to share with people who were not present.

4. The **structure** of the story is: 10–15-minute presentation to the village, any format you feel appropriate (dance, poetry, rap, music, video, painting, PowerPoint), must have a title and cannot be about everything you experienced, just the most important to you, the teacher will provide (technology, etc.) the rest is up to you.

5. For **clarity** purposes: the way in which you tell your story is an important part of the story—be creative. Ten minutes is a long time in front of people, so make sure to time your story in rehearsals. This is 100% about your response to our guest speaker—what you feel and think are the only things that matter. Research material you are unsure of. We are engaging in this exercise to collect your responses so that we can define a theme for our story.

6. After the assignment has been explained and there are no more questions, open up the village to a a brief heart-storming session. This will relive those who were worried about 'doing it right' and provide useful vocabulary for all of them to proceed.

7. Give a strict due date. You will not have time to see every My Story in one class meeting, so create a sign-up sheet for who goes when. Provide 5-10 minutes of discussion time following each *My Story*.

While the *My Story* assignment is being worked on by your students outside of class, this will be a good time to define and practice the village building games and exercises during class time. When the presentations are ready to be shared with the village....

8. Ask the students how the *My Story* work went for them. Remind them that these are not small Broadway shows, simply applied research for our story building work together. Remind them we will engage in village response sessions following each *My Story*; Village Rules apply.

9. Be mindful of everything that surfaces during these sessions. Again, it is the stuff that your village's story is made of and may surface outside of expected areas (i.e. discussions, debates).

10. Write the title of each *My Story* on the board. Ask the village after each presentation "How does the title reflect the story?" and "How are story titles similar to themes?"

11. Once every student in the village has presented their *My Story*, you should have a board filled with titles/themes.

12. Ask the village if they see any trends, patterns, relationships with the titles/themes. Ask the village to place the related titles/themes into groups.

13. Ask the students to choose one group (family) of titles/themes they feel the strongest connection too. Select 3-5 (depending on class size) locations around the room and identify each location as one of the title/theme groups; ask students to go to the location they are drawn too. (You may have to balance and equalize the groups a bit).

14. Ask each group to discuss the multiple titles/themes in their group. Ask them to create one theme (not title) that best represents the group they are a part of. (10 minutes).

15. Clap the groups back to the village. Share each group's theme work, discuss.

16. Return to the collaborative groups—wordsmith if necessary. Assignment: Physically and abstractly communicate this theme for the village. Move the content from the *brain to the body to the heart*...it should be noisy! (10-15 minutes.)

After the groups have had sufficient time, clap them back to the village.

17. Ask the village how this collaborative process went for them. Which village rules were applied, which ignored? Ask them to finish this sentences: "That collaborative process worked best when we _____," and "That collaborative process stopped when we _____." Saying these ideas aloud is important as it moves the *knowing* to *doing*.

18. Remind them of the importance of moving the work from the *brain to the body to the heart.*

19. Remind them of the breathing rhythm emulated in the collaborative village process.

20. Ask which group would like to share first. Each group shares their physical theme with the village and says the theme only after they have abstractly expressed it.

21. Ask the rest of the village to respond to each group's theme. Village Rules apply during feedback sessions.

22. After all of the groups have shared and received village feedback, refocus on just the themes and ask the village to make observations regarding repetition, patterns, language and sequences. What do they **feel**?

23. Keep each group's theme they just shared on the board.

24. As a village, heart storm until **one theme** surfaces from those remaining on the board. It can be a combination of themes left or words borrowed from one to plug into another. This will be the **theme** of your story.

25. Keep the heart storming theme boards: My Story titles and themes, etc. These will be helpful to refer to throughout the process. Take photos of the boards.

AFP Student-Artist facilitating a Story Build: THEME

Congratulations! Your village now has the 'what' of their story, the **Theme**. Be prepared for the observation, "All that for this?!" The answer is an unapologetically "Yes." You and your students have just enacted a core principle of story building: In order for an event to become meaningful and engaging in performance, it must be squeezed, filtered and pressed through the village so only its most essential elements remain. This economical product is the *truth* of the story. You will keep all the messy pages and boards filled with words, themes, and ideas as they will be valuable resources and research for the village later in the process. The process thus far is not unlike a swimmer who is preparing for their next big meet. They will spend hours and hours in the pool, often alone, altering, defining, and perfecting their technique. When they finally get to the competition the audience witnesses them for (hopefully) just minutes or seconds. The audience is not cheering for the boring complete narrative leading to this moment, they are cheering for the economical story in front of them—the race—the *theme*.

Your theme is the litmus test for every moment ahead in the story building process. As the creativity of the village expresses itself at full strength, you must bring the students back to the task at hand. The story will be pushed and pulled in multiple, fascinating directions—which road should the village follow? The answer must always refer to the *theme*. Does the present direction we are moving towards directly connect to our theme? Will this choice inform our theme? Is this moment helpful in supporting our theme? These are excellent questions to reflect on as the creativity bubbles with excitement. If the answers to the above questions are 'Yes,' then continue on the present path. If the village cannot connect the work to the *theme*, stop and reload. As I discussed earlier, you will write several stories during this process, but only one will survive. Discarding ideas that do not support the *theme* does not mean they weren't amazing ideas. It means they, simply, do not support the *theme*, that's all. Keep these discarded ideas in your resource library—they will be great for future stories. Post the village's theme clearly in your workspace, review it often, refer to it regularly, be proud of it...you've earned it.

THEME Board

"A good head and good heart are always a formidable combination. But when you add to that a literate tongue, then you have something very special."

Nelson Mandela

The Story Building Process
Act III: Shaping the Story

ow you know the **Theme** or the *What* of your story; *what* lesson your story will be teaching. You and the village also practiced the village rules to create something for the first time—that's no small task, well done! Your village will come bounding into class, proud of their theme, willingly throw themselves into what now should be a more efficient circle preparation, and then stare at you with high expectations... So.... now...what? (awkward silence—lots of looking around, deer in headlights, etc.) Next step...**Structure!**

Structure = the 'Who,' 'Where' and 'Why' of the Story

How does this bumper sticker become a story to share? The short answer: more hard work. The longer answer: the next step in the story building process is to create the internal language of the story, the *structure* of the story. If the theme is the **What** of the story, the structure is the **Who, Where** and **Why** of the story: *Who* is the story about *Where* is this event happening and *Why* are they here? The **Who** are all the characters in your story—your protagonists, antagonists and contrasting characters. These need not be people, and I always urge my students to consider people as the last option for their characters. Imagining objects (mountains, water, cars), ideas (freedom, time, education) and feelings (anger, fear, pleasure) as possible characters initially will start this step of the process with open theatricality. When we begin with people, we, ironically, limit their future possibilities and experiences. This returns us to the power of abstraction vs. literalness in performance. The **Where** of the story are the physical locations of the events of the story as well as the 'world' of the play. The physical locations (outer space, a jungle, the ocean) inform the event in multiple obvious ways. The 'world' of the play includes the nuanced details of the physical locations that not only color the physical place (a dense jungle dripping with moisture, insects, and rare fruit), but also the emotional details of the location (a jungle bursting with life and excitement having just survived another harsh dry season, happy to be alive). As the teacher, asking your students for adjectives always works well. "Using only single adjectives, describe the jungle in our story?" More word lists, you're correct! The **Why** of the story is the reason and purpose of the **Who** and the **Where**— **Why** are they here? For what event have they assembled in this particular place? Remember, meaningful stories are not common, low staked events…they are special occurrences that deserve to be shared so valuable lessons can be learned. Stories are, unique experiences where the *What, Who, Where and Why* meet to create some fireworks worth watching. Certainly, just defining the *Who, Where* and *Why* of the story does not a story make. For now, keep the above information in mind, remember to stay abstract for as long as possible and ask for adjectives. We will return to coloring the story with the *Who, Where* and *Why* soon, but we need the coloring book, the lines, shapes, and outlines to color in—we need the blanks to fill in. We cannot release our characters into their environments without direction—they need a road map. This road map is called *structure* in story building. If we are in fact building a story here (last metaphor, I promise) we must create the framing of the building before we slap up walls, paint, and fixtures. If we were to add these architectural details without the supporting structure underneath, the building would collapse—so is the case with story. If we were to send our characters into the jungle without structure, they would run about aimlessly until their journeys collapsed. Structure is essential for building meaningful stories.

Continuing the kinesthetic commitment while exploring **STRUCTURE.**

The Science Behind Story Structure

"I am watching an amazing neural ballet in which a story line changes the activity of people's brains."—Paul J. Zak

Neuroscientist Paul Zak's research on how story structure impacts the brain is important to our conversation. His laboratory has demystified the reasons we feel certain ways after being engaged in stories with clear dramatic arcs and structure. As his research subjects watched a fictional story about a father spending the final remaining days with his dying son, they found two chemicals were released in the brain. Cortisol, which focuses our attention on something important and correlates, in this story, to the distress the father feels for his son. The second chemical was oxytocin that is associated with care, connection, and empathy. Distress and Empathy are important for social creatures because they allow us to understand how others are reacting to challenging situations. Empathy is also amongst the most difficult yet sought after attributes to teach—we hear this time and time again form the teachers we work with. We also find that teachers run from distress. This is crazy to me! Life is filled with distress, so isn't it our job in the schools to provide tools and vocabulary for our students to deal with distress? I find suffering to be underrated. We never stop our students from feeling joy, let's not stop them from feeling distress. We also know that the brain releases a third chemical when experiencing an emotionally charged event, Dopamine, which makes it easier to remember the story and with greater accuracy. So, when we really feel the pain and joys of the characters in a good story we are not just 'softies' looking for tissues, we are victims of being human—victims of science. It is interesting to note in Zak's research that when subjects were shown stories with poor dramatic structure they were not engaged and therefore their brains did not release cortisol or oxytocin. Stories need to be told well to be effective. Telling stories well has something to do with the actors, sets and costumes, but much more to do with story structure. Structure is the silent player in the story world—we are comforted when it is there and bored when its not. The sequencing, patterns and repeated milestones all provide valuable information to our subconscious, giving us the security to align ourselves with the protagonist's journey. You would never experience a meaningful story and report "Excellent structure!" Well, you might know now that we have pulled the structure from its subliminal home into the conscious world. You will soon see the importance of structure, the value in teaching it to your student and why we must apply it to our story building process. You would never walk into an office building if you knew there were no supportive framing holding the building up in space—it would be foolish and dangerous. The same is true for story—don't allow your students to walk into the story building process without structure—foolish and dangerous indeed.

There was a popular child psychology experiment done with preschoolers in the 1970's. While the research question was not about story structure, its findings does reveal the importance of structure in our lives. A group of 20 preschoolers were brought to a playground. These children had never met before. The playground was typically equipped with the necessities: swings, slides, jungle gym, monkey bars. Surrounding the circumference of the playground was a ten-foot fence. The children were released into the playground. By and large, this groups of preschool strangers played quite well together, taking turns, waiting in lines, collaborating for make believe games and assisting each other when necessary. One week later the same group of children were brought to the same playground. Everything was the same with one exception: The perimeter fence has been removed. This was not announced to the children, and they were released to play again. Things did not go so well this time: there was bickering, fighting, impatience, a distinct lack of cooperation and very few successful collaborations. Did one student stand up and say "Bring back the fence so we can play nicely again!" Of course not. The students were not consciously aware of the fence being removed...but it certainly impacted their behavior. Their subconscious security had been removed, so they no longer felt safe. The psychological comfort the structure had provided was gone, so they acted accordingly. Structure in story provides the same comfort, the same security the same confidence for our audiences. When structure is strong, consistent, and well crafted, the audience is willing to be patient, cooperate and collaborate. When the structure is weak or non-existent, the audience, like the preschoolers, will grow impatient, insecure, and uncooperative. Reflect on this idea as teachers and parents. What an amazing opportunity to teach this important life lesson through the medium of story!

While there are many story structures, I will share a few that have been especially effective with the AFP work and seem to resonate most clearly with high school and university students.

The Climactic Structure or Dramatic Arc

The dramatic arc that Zak refers to in his work is a simple story structure we are all familiar with at the subconscious level—it looks like this:

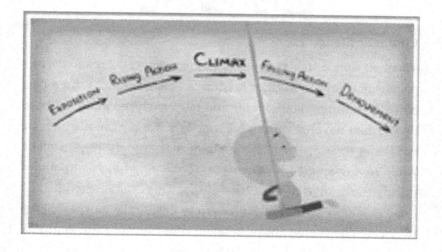

Neuroscience and Dramatic Structure—
Scan to view video

Climactic Structure

The next simple structure has been given many titles and derives primarily from the work of Aristotle's Poetics and the three-part plot (Beginning, Middle, End) and later analyzed and processed by German novelist Gustav Freytag as a five-part plot which we now refer to as Freytag's Pyramid, or more simply, the Dramatic Arc. Freytag applied his theory to the five-act plays so popular during the dramas of the 19th century. This dramatic (climactic) arc can supply structure for a variety of literary journeys, long or short. The image above is taken directly from the Paul Zak research—that's the cute little boy who is dying from cancer in the story on the swing. A more traditional image of the dramatic or climactic arc is here:

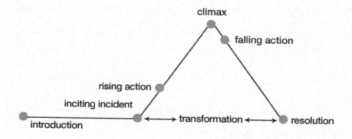

Take your students on a story-structure stroll through this structure using a story they all know. Ask them to list the elements within each structure segment:

The Little Mermaid

Exposition/Introduction/Stasis

What do we know? Ariel is a mermaid who lives in the sea, her father is King of the sea, she has friends named Sebastian and flounder, she has a beautiful singing voice, she longs for more, is habitually late, etc.

Inciting Incident/MDQ

Ariel does the one thing every mermaid/man is forbidden to do, go to the water's surface where she sees Prince Eric and falls in love...Boom, off we go, the inciting incident has propelled Ariel into her dramatic arc, stasis has been broken, The MDQ: Will Ariel live happily ever after with Eric?

Rising Action

On Ariel's quest to answer the MDQ she encounters multiple conflicts and obstacles: Ursula the Sea Witch, her father's anger, her communities' expectations, the difficult decision to trade her voice for human legs, etc. These problems get larger and more numerous the further she travels up the rising action. The problems have reached a feverish pitch at the decisive, explosive decision to sacrifice everything she knows for the chance to be with Eric for the rest of her life…

Climax

In an epic and glorious scene, Ariel trades her voice for human legs, Triton and Ursula engage in a magical battle….

Falling Action

Ursula has been extinguished, Triton retains his kingdom, gives Ariel and Eric his blessing., etc. Important: The falling action is MUCH shorter than the rising action. This is crucial because it emphasizes the universal story truth that we have endless desire for conflict, problems and obstacles, and extremely limited patience for things going well. In this case the geometry of the dramatic arc (climactic structure) is completely wrong in most pictures. The rising action should be a long, extended line on its way to the climax, but the falling action should be much shorter on its way to journey's end—these lines are NOT equal. If they are, you will lose your audience. What typically happens during the falling actin of a film? The credits!

Resolution/Denouement

The theme music gets louder, Eric and Ariel are magically changed into their wedding clothes, Triton waves goodbye, etc. All is well. We have returned to stasis.

Transformation

If the stasis at the end of the story is the same as the stasis in the beginning of the story, we, as story-builders, have failed. What happens on that all mighty arc must be significant enough to change stasis forever; a transformation has occurred. If the transformation in stasis improves upon the original stasis, we call the story a 'comedy.' If the transformation in stasis damages and reduces the original stasis, we call the story a 'tragedy.' Transformation happens to the world of the story (Atlantis) and the characters who travelled on the dramatic arc (Ariel, Triton, Ursula). Well-structured stories transform the characters in a story so profoundly, that they offer the audience an opportunity to transform as well.

The Hero's Journey

The concept of the archetypical 'Hero's Journey' surfaces regularly throughout the scholarship of Joseph Campbell. After you have read (or viewed) his seminal *The Power of Myth*, I highly recommend his *Hero With a Thousand Faces*. Campbell suggests we are the *hero* of our individual life journeys, suffering fire-breathing dragons and reaping pots of gold as we navigate the complex tests life puts before us. I suppose Campbell might argue with my 'complex' description, as he has a unique ability to whittle down each journey segment to simple, shared experiences that will seem obvious and even expected. When I share this structure option with my students they always respond with "I wish someone would have shown this to me when I started high school—it would have saved me so much time and frustration!" Like the climactic structure, this cycle (circular) structure already lives in each of us innately. While you may not have articulated this structure as we are about to, you certainly are familiar with it—from sacred, religious texts, to popular films, to classic novels, to how we each live our lives, the hero's journey is familiar on multiple levels.

Take your students on a story-structure stroll through the Hero's Journey using a story they all know; let's use shared life experience this time. Ask them to list the elements within each structure segment:

Going to College

(I have found this experience to surface immensely important discussions and conversations. You may also want to use 'High School' or 'Adolescence.' Guidance counselors should hand a Hero's Journey image to every student they meet with—I have one for you in this chapter)

Call to Adventure

It's time to leave the comfort of your *Known*: high school, home-town, your family, friends, etc. and take that scary leap into that *Unknown* adventure called college! You may have procrastinated as you filled out applications and mourned the future loss of the familiar. It is typical for the hero to reject the call initially, but the call will keep coming; the pressure to attend college is intense, a rite of passage.

Supernatural Aid

This is the 'call helper,' and can be society, family legacy, god, your inner voice, the connecting with someone/something special during a campus visit, etc. The spiritual boost to answer the call. This person/entity can also be referred to as the *Herald*.

Threshold (Guardians)

Transitioning from the *Known* to the *Unknown* is scary for you and everyone who knows you. *Threshold Guardians* are people, beings, or situations which block the hero's passage into the unknown world part of their journey. High school friends who are staying close to home, overly protective relatives, society suggesting you aren't smart enough, etc.

Known/Unknown

Moving from the *known* to the *unknown* is the essential leap that must occur to propel the hero into the story, the journey. In the Climactic Structure the *known* = *stasis* and the *threshold (to the unknown)* = *inciting incident*. As you can see the hero's journey is a circle, cyclical in nature, meaning it (our life journeys) are a continuum, we are never 'finished,' thus the *unknown* will become *known* through the journey—your *known* will expand as your adventures expand. You will always be invited to experience new *unknowns*—you may know people who never answer their calls to adventure and stay locked in their *knowns* forever—how would you describe these people? Fear and courage are important ideas to consider when moving from the *known* to the *unknown*...this is challenging stuff!

Helper #1

You have left home, your parents have dropped you off at your dorm, and you are trying your best not to look as terrified as you feel. As you walk across this foreign land with shaky legs to your first orientation meeting a voice from behind you asks "Hey, you need help finding where you are going?" The orientation leader was you last year, her unknown has become more known, and she has appeared to *help* you on your journey.

Mentor

College is not the 13th grade, its filled with multiple challenges and temptations (coming up next) that nobody told you about. Your heightened expectations can be overwhelming, you need someone to fill in the blanks for you...a *Mentor*. This can take the shape of a professor, counselor, coach, advisor, or advanced student. The *mentor's* assistance is more in-depth and long-term than the *helper*. The *mentor* can be returned to multiple times for assistance, advice and wisdom—their job is to help you move forward on your journey, keep you on your path, etc.

Challenges and Temptations

Like conflicts and obstacles, *challenges* and *temptations* are what make the hero's journey interesting to watch. For the hero, *challenges* and *temptations* are often arduous, painful and uncomfortable. The fire breathing dragons and Lord Voldemorts are replaced with intense academic responsibilities, expanded freedom, college parties, financial pressures, joining clubs, fitting in, etc. College is, in fact, one of the most *challenging unknowns* to experience filled with a minefield of *temptations*. When you think of the hundreds of thousands of new heroes who plunge into this unknown every year it's no wonder graduation rates are so poor—fighting these battles is a tall order and sometimes (too often) the dragon wins.

Helper #2

Right around the middle of the college journey, just when the hero has become adept at meeting the *challenges* and balancing the *temptations* a new, larger, higher staked *challenge* surfaces. Just when the hero was feeling more *known* in their *unknown*, Bam! This helper will surface to assist the hero in pulling it together. Again, a friend, classmate, sorority sister, teammate will take on this responsibility.

Abyss (Death/Rebirth)

This new, intensified challenge, this two-headed monster of a problem can take the shape of being denied entrance into a specialized program, being rejected by a significant other, diminished financial support or falling on academic probation—yikes! Despite the assistance of the *helper*, the magnitude of the **loss** the hero is experiencing will make them feel stuck and incapable of moving forward. The hero is in a dark, lonely place: he *Abyss*. There is a way out of the *abyss*—something must be released, given up — something must die so the hero can move forward on their journey, to live. For so many of my past students, the equation is painfully (literally) simple: Their 'big kid' must die so their 'young adult' can live. The *loss* that tossed the hero into the *abyss* is a lesson wrapped in pain—*the loss is the death required to live*. (Wow! Crucial, important, essential life lesson. It will make your stories better too).

Revelation

The sudden dramatic change in the way the hero thinks or views life. It usually comes in the form of a forced action or an epiphany in which the hero "realizes" they can move forward even after (or because of) suffering the loss in the abyss. This 'aha' moment is the ticket out of the abyss—the truth is 'revealed' to the hero which provides the energy necessary to thrust her forward, continuing her heroic journey. The hero has realized the loss was necessary to her evolution—no small lesson and the real reason to go to college—tuition at work!

Transformation

This is the part where the old character "dies" so the new part of the hero can be born. The hero is now very different from what he was in the beginning (Freshman) of the story because the hero has learned the required lessons (Sophomore) from the mentor and other helpers. The hero has new enthusiasm (Junior), sees what must be done (commits to major, travels abroad), and is eager to confront the problem (Senior year—Graduation). Actually, transformation begins as soon as the threshold is crossed—the unknown of college slowly peels away the layers of known through a vulnerable, challenging four-year journey.

Atonement

The hero is fully changed, is at peace with the "new" self. The hero accepts his/her singular responsibility to solve the problem or "rights the wrong" and fulfills the role created by destiny—a college graduate! The hero saves the day and restores safety and security—she is prepared for her future armed with an undergraduate degree, symbolizing the multiple *challenges* and *temptations* she had to overcome. Perhaps all university diplomas should have fire-breathing dragons on them?

Return to the Known

The character returns to the *known* world to many accolades. He is happier, wiser, honored, and respected. The hero receives the "Gift of the Goddess" by getting a promotion, receiving a medal or a celebratory parade. In traditional hero journeys the hero receives the beautiful princess' hand in marriage ('gift of goddess') for saving the *known*—the village and its inhabitants. When the freshly decreed college-graduate returns home the gift may be respect, employment, a car, clothing, a new home, or a key to the city! Many college graduate hero's report returning to their *known* is far less positive than expected—their journey has changed them and their *known* forever. Thomas Wolfe's novel title *You Can't Go Home Again* is a profound comment on the dangerous truth of personal growth.

The Power of the Circle

As I have mentioned throughout this section, the life lessons reflected in the *Hero's Journey* are abundant. I have experienced multiple profoundly important discussions with my students when introducing this story structure. They are immediately hooked on its power and, most importantly, its emphasis on their favorite subject, themselves! Education is (should be) much more about students learning to listen to their hearts and identifying their spirits than listening to lectures and identifying facts. The story-building process presents multiple opportunities for you to engage your students in authentic contemplative learning experiences that will contribute to their life journeys. As we unpack the *Hero's Journey*, it is easy to cut/paste the hero's experiences with student life experiences. Thus, the journey is indeed a microcosm for your student's lives. Perhaps even more poignant is the macro lesson reflected in the overall shape of the *Hero's Journey*—the **circle**. The circle of the journey reflects the cycle, the continuum of life. As we return to the *known* and are showered with praise, a few more steps along the top arc of the circle places us at yet another *threshold* to a new *unknown*. Yes, life is one hero journey after another! There is a giant 'if' however. Accepting the *call to adventure* is not mandatory and requires immense courage. I agree with Campbell's theory that everyone is offered multiple *Hero Journeys* throughout their life. Those who accept the call to adventure experience the authentic evolution and growth of what it means to be alive—they 'follow their bliss.' Unfortunately, most people refuse their *call to adventures* and remain in the *known* their entire life. As you review the *Hero's Journey* diagram above, trace with your finger the part of the circle encompassing the *known*—back and forth, back and forth. This path ignores most of the available circle, or as Campbell would suggest, this path ignores the true purpose of our presence on this planet, thus personal bliss will be unattainable. While dramatic elements of the hero's journey will differ quite a bit from story to story, a shared character trait of all hero's remains constant: **Courage**. If you can impart the importance of courage in life with your students during the Hero's Journey discussion, you have done them a great service.

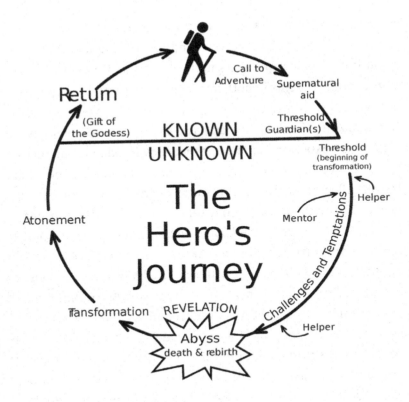

Keepin' it Simple Structure

STORY STRUCTURE

ONCE UPON A TIME THERE WAS _____   EVERY DAY _____

ONE DAY _____   BECAUSE OF THAT _____

BECAUSE OF THAT _____   UNTIL FINALLY _____

A third story structure option is a simple one and always a winner with students. It is simple because of its brevity and clarity—they know how to fill in the blank! It's a winner for two reasons: First, as you've already learned, because their brains are wired for this expected sequence and important pattern—you may actually hear audible sighs of relief when your students first see this. Secondly, it's a winner because it is the magic recipe for all of Pixar's animated features. Just plug *A Bug's Life, Toy Story, Finding Nemo* or *Wall-E* into the blanks and, poof, you too have the story power! You have drunk the mighty Pixar elixir and are intoxicated with its simple power. Once again, as with all our story structures, we have surfaced a dusty chunk of knowledge from your subconscious library to unpack, examine and play with. The beauty of this process is, after we have consciously explored these structures, when we do return them to our subconscious they are fully realized and sharply defined—we have blown off the dust, cleaned and clarified important information with intention and purpose, thus making it more available for future use.

Take your students on a story-structure stroll through the Pixar structure using a story they all know. Ask them to simply fill in the blanks.

Toy Story

Once Upon A Time There Was: *a young boy named Andy who loved his toys.*

Every Day: *he played with his favorite toy Woody, a cowboy doll.*

One Day: *Andy's parents decide to move and buy him a Buzz Lightyear action figure.*

Because Of That: *Woody felt his position as favorite toy was jeopardized.*

Because Of That: *Woody and Buzz struggle to remain Andy's favorite toys and stay clear of the evil next door neighbor Sid during the move.*

** You can add as many 'Because Of That's' as you need**

Until Finally: *Woody and Buzz reunite with Andy and the other toys in their new house and escape Sid's evil plans, to live happily ever after.*

I never share this simple story structure as first option. The students would be fooled into the false belief that it's easier than the others. This structure works well as the roadmap for the entire story, or, for specific, smaller sections of the story as you begin piecing the elements together in smaller applied research groups. This simple structure also works well to help smaller groups get going when they believe they are stuck. Keep this simple structure handy—it will become an important utility for you throughout the process.

Global Teaching Opportunity

Because of the immense popularity of Hollywood and Broadway, there is a false assumption (or is it arrogance?) that the whole world tells stories like us in the West. This is untrue. We certainly have embraced the idea of linear story telling where predictable sequences and patterns abound. We like this comfort and, based on the neural research, we have every right to feel this sense of security. The United States is a baby country, and we should be proud of American contributions to the world in such a relatively short period of time. In many ways, the American genius lies in our ability to gather expertise from around the globe and process it as new—a true reflection of the diverse community that is the U.S. The climactic and Hero's story structures exist all over the world to be sure. Elements of the Hero's journey can be traced to every corner of our globe—Joseph Campbell shares thrilling examples of this 'sameness' throughout his work. The same stories and rituals are being shared by communities who have never encountered each other—they are instinctively following their bliss. However, this idea that stories *must* follow a singular line of action, a logical thought process, a linear model for delivering stories is untrue and very Western-centric. The story world does not revolve around this newish country called the United States of America. In fact, elaborate traditions of story sharing have existed for thousands of years outside of the Americas.

Take for instance the internal dynamics of Japanese stories where characters goals take a back seat to the pursuit of virtues encompassed by events. The road to these virtues is often on the heels of the antagonist not the protagonist and time passage is more symbolic than literal:

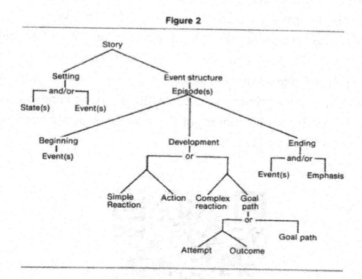

Figure 2

Or consider the West African folktales where animals and nature are the central vehicles for learning valuable answers to life questions like "Why is the sky blue?" and life lessons like "Respect the words of your elders." These delightful anecdotes were passed on from generation to generation—when Grandma announced it was time for a story, it wasn't to be entertained, it was to accept valuable life lessons. A central character in many of these stories was the troublesome and tricky spider Anansi. Anansi is on constant display throughout these tales as his selfishness and greed show us how **not** to behave. Unlike Western expectations, Anansi is never punished to illustrate his mistake—his mistake is the illustration, and he lives on to make future mistakes for the good of humanity. Hundreds of Anansi stories still exist—their titles (i.e. *The Lion and the Snake*) are always the same, but what happens between the beginning and end of these stories differs based on the **telling** of the story. West African folktales are always spoken as, historically, their audiences were illiterate. The oral component is crucial—so crucial that those special people in the village whose job it was to impart the great wisdom of these stories were revered at the highest level. They were thought of as magic priests rather than entertainers. These 'Griots' were responsible for teaching the children of the village so that correct histories and life lessons could be handed to future generations. So, while there is an unashamed joy in the delivery, the content of these stories was serious stuff (scan below for video).

Anansi's 'spiderness' can take several forms and qualities, but his lesson-bound purpose remains constant as you will note in this wonderful video:

Since stories happen all over the world, and these stories reflect the communities they serve, they are ideal global teaching opportunities for you and your students. As you know, stories offer an economical, compressed reflection of the events they share, so they become perfect vehicles for multiple lessons. In a day and age when teaching diversity, multiculturalism and global influences is more of a priority than ever; where teachers are clamoring for teachable, concise content to squeeze within their shrinking time with students, international story structures and styles can be important curricular vehicles. Story *style* is the *how* of the storytelling; how will we deliver the story to our audience, what will be the *style* of performance (music, puppetry, expressionism, etc.)? We will investigate *style* in detail in the next chapter, but I mention it here because it will offer you a greater array of global teaching opportunities than story structure.

Choosing the Best Structure for Your Story

The relationship between **Theme** (*What*) and **Structure** (*Who, Where, Why*) and your overall story is significant. You will need to dig deeply here with your students as they will, more often than not, choose the structure they are most familiar with. This will translate as using the climatic structure over and over again. There is nothing wrong of course with using this structure; it is important that the village come to it as a result of justified heart-storming, discussion and research. Why choose one over another? Here are some possible questions to ask the village to ignite this important discussion:

- Is it a question of tempo, rhythm or movement?

- Is it a question of providing for exterior instead of interior locations?

- Will one structure provide for character needs better than another?

- Will one structure encompass the sense of conflict better than the other?

- Which structure will provide for greater overall story clarity?

- Which structure will be most helpful for the audience in identifying the theme?

Here's the great thing about these discussions: You really can't go wrong with the questions. As long as your questions encourage the students to justify their choices based on the needs of the story, you are asking the 'right' questions. The most important element is not the eventual story structure chosen—rather, the most important element is having the discussion guided by the Village Rules, thus further defining the village, thus (you got it) further defining the story. It is not enough to extract one-word answers from your students during this discussion. The follow up questions to each of your questions are:

- Why was that your response?

- Share specific examples directly supporting our story.

#Breadcrumb Alert#

The Wiggle Effect

*This is an important moment to identify throughout the process with your students. After necessarily lengthy discussion sessions where theory, context and heartstorming are shared, you will know when your students have had enough; their brains are full and it's time to move theory-to-action. Their scientifically tested, universally shared signal to you, their teacher, is **the wiggle**. OK, maybe not scientifically tested, but universally expressed for sure! Derived, I believe, from the preschool 'I have to go potty but don't want to leave what I'm doing' dance, the wiggle is a repeated, staccato movement of the foot, torso, or pelvis that screams 'I need to move!' If you attempt to punish these impulses by ignoring them and attempt to cram more information into your student's heads, you will be sorely disappointed.*

*Not only will they be unable to process the information, they will completely ignore you. I have come to the conclusion that my students must in fact **earn the wiggle** by engaging in intelligent, in-depth, respectful discussions and heartstorming.*

Theory-to-Action

Break into Collaborative Groups

Now that the village has been exposed to a variety of story structures and their importance, and they have discussed reasoning for choosing one or another, they are ready to activate theory. Again, and I cannot say this enough, the final step in making the best choice(s) for your stories is to experiment options through your student's bodies. This physical litmus test will clearly and immediately separate what you may have thought would be the best choice, from what is truly best for the story. If I had a dollar for every time the village was 'sure' of their post discussion choice, only to discover it was something different after putting the options through their bodies, I would be a rich man. A simple phrase in my teaching arsenal I use frequently to steer the village to a community truth when it is at an impasse, is: "I don't know the answer, let's *see* it before we make a decision." The shoe company Nike has it right, "Just Do It!"

Our brains lie to us all the time—we know that its proven. So why would we stop at simply *knowing* with any process? This would suggest (and has of course) that we are simply thinking machines devoid of feelings, emotions, and tactile experiences. The Contemplative learning folks would argue that no idea is fully realized until it has been introduced to the breath, body and spirit. Why is this idea considered so 'odd' in contemporary education arenas? Why is the idea of including the whole person in the learning process deemed 'novel' or 'innovative?' This idea should be happening in every classroom in our country; as we walk down the hallways of American schools, we should be witnessing sweaty students jumping, stretching and exploring ideas with their bodies...loudly! That would mean we are listening to the research and are providing the appropriate environment for student learning. That would be an exhilarating school visit in comparison to the tip-toeingly silent hallways that presently dominate our school landscapes. I have two short stories to share with you before I descend from this soapbox and guide you through the next exercises.

First story: While at local high school years ago, the state education representatives were conducting their annual site visit to assess the work being done. Several well-dressed folks with their clipboards marched down the hallways together peering in and out of rooms, taking notes, and sharing important whispers with each other. This particular school was extremely traditional in its learning models and everyone (students, faculty, staff) had been briefed the day before by the school's principal—above all else, the message of following orders and being polite was emphasized. At the end of the visit the leader of the state education group commended the principal on the school's behavior and said "We are especially impressed by how well-mannered your students are—everywhere we went they were so still and quiet, just lovely!" The lesson: Quite and still is good and to be rewarded. The truth: Even though we know this is not the ideal way to educate students and guarantee authentic learning, it is EASIER for schools to manage students by enforcing silence and stillness. As you can imagine, I have had several meetings with the principal of this school since that visit sharing my thoughts—we have not been invited to return.

Second story: While in residence at a local high school whose population is 100% New Americans (students who are from other countries who have been in the U.S. two years or less), my/our job was to bring DBE and AFP story-building to the teachers, students, and administrators. As you might imagine, emphasizing the use of body with the students was a primary focus of ours as we attempted to find universal communication options—there are over 50 languages spoken at this school. Because we were consistently present in the school, the teachers and staff had access to us for application suggestions and they were eager to apply the work. The school eagerly applied the use of story at every level possible—this is a value and objective of the school and is becoming its very ethos. The state education folks were scheduled to make their assessment visit one day—the suits and clipboards in tow, they walked through the hallways of this school. Rather than trying to make less noise with their heels, they bumped into a group of students who were hurriedly moving out of their social studies classroom searching for a larger space to do their work. Their teacher was working on a concept whose western context baffled the students, so he confessed to them "I don't know the answer, let's see it before we make a decision." Once they found an open space in the hallway, the students, guided by their teacher, physically expressed their emotional responses to the ideas that confused them in class. One light bulb ignited after another (you could literally see each student light up and get it!), the students celebrated with each other by shared hugs, high-fives and laughs and stormed back into class. The teacher looked back at the principal with a mix of pride and fear before rejoining his students in their room. There was a wonderfully awkward silence, the principal courageously ready for any questions—he was a major proponent of story-based learning. One state education representative broke the silence "What was that?!" Before the principal could explain a young-ish member of the state education pack responded, "That looked like real, fun, and exciting learning to me." There were assorted grunts of agreement and confusion as they pressed on with their hallway journey. In the end the state education folks commended the school's use of 'non-traditional learning to accommodate the non-traditional students.' While I agreed with the principal that he was a victim of a back handed compliment, I also reminded him that change is hard, and these folks were not used to change. Sticking to the way things have been done in the past is **easy** and the most **convenient** option which is why it's the preferred path. Changing the paradigm if how and why we teach is **difficult** and requires immense **time, effort** and **courage**, which is why it's not the preferred path. I wish the central obstacle to transforming our educational system were more complicated than that but its not. We made a crack in the firm armor of traditional education that day—a crack, I reminded our forward-thinking principal, that will eventually grow to the wide-open norm of how we teach *every* student. AFP is contracted to remain in residence at this wonderful school through 2020.

OK, time for you and your village to 'Just Do It" with the following theory-to-action exercises as you choose the best possible structure for your story.

Theory-to-Action

Step 1: Three-Word Structure Stories

1. At the culmination of your structure choice discussion remind the village "I don't know the answer, let's see it before we make a decision." (or your version).

2. As an entire village, choose three words they all believe as vital to the story thus far (i.e. Truth, Strength, Mountain).

3. Point to three areas of the room identified by the story structure options (i.e Climactic to the right corner, Hero's Journey to the left corner, etc.). Ask the students to go to the area they feel most strongly as the best choice for their story. Have as many groups as you have structures presented—three is a good number to focus on. Remind the village that group selection should be based entirely on what is best for the story not who you'd like to be with, etc. Village Rules continues to guide the actions of the village.

4. Group assignment: Using your chosen structure as your guide, prepare a short story to share with the rest of the village including the three-words just chosen. These words can be incorporated in any way the group chooses. No words can be spoken, all communications must only use bodies and voices of your group. Reminders: Stay abstract, be brave, commit to your ideas fully and you must have fun. Exercise Objective: Searching for the best possible

structure for our story by physically experimentation. (10 minutes)

5. As you move about the room (teacher) remind the groups that it is important to emphasize the elements of their chosen structure they just learned. Illustrating the structure is the focus of this exercise. Being physical, vocal, and creative in your exploration of structure is much more important than being 'right.' There is not 'right/wrong' since they are creating these for the first time—if they are fully committed and collaborative, they are doing it 'right.'

#Breadcrumb Alert#

While emphasizing one element to define the lesson in a particular exercise, other elements can/must diminish. This is important as it releases the students from the pressure to be great all the time at everything—this is impossible and unrealistic. It cannot be 'game time' all the time—this is a difficult concept for students to practice. During football practice the coach will take the players through specific drills to refine a certain element of the game needing attention—to enhance speed, the players might be asked to move quickly through multiple cones arranged in an obstacles course. The players are not playing football, they don't even have a ball! The players will incorporate their newfound speed on game day, not during practice. The players catching ability will diminish during these speed drills because that's not what they are working on. Consider all of our physical work during the story-building process as practice or Rehearsal—there's a reason we don't invite audiences to practices in sports or rehearsals in the arts—it 'aint pretty! While emphasizing story structure, character details will suffer; while emphasizing story environment, character relationships will suffer...that's great!

Applaud this willingness to place one idea above the surface while allowing everything else to swim about below the surface. Not only will this develop detailed focus techniques with your students, but it will also contribute mightily to the success of your story-building. Publicly address and respond to this idea whenever possible—cheer your players loudly as they move through the cones!

6. After the groups have had sufficient time, clap them back to the village.

7. Ask the village how this collaborative process went for them. Which village rules were applied, which ignored. Ask them to finish this sentence: "That collaborative process worked best when we _____," and "That collaborative process stopped when we _____." Saying these ideas aloud is important as it moves the *knowing* to *doing*. Did they notice improvement from the last time they broke into collaborative groups? Their movement from the village to the collaborative groups and back to the village will get smoother each time—it will eventually become second nature. This will happen sooner than you think—announcing their successes will accelerate the process.

8. Remind them of the importance of moving the work from the *brain to the body to the heart*.

9. Remind them of the breathing rhythm emulated in the collaborative village process.

10. Each group shares their physical structure story with the village—each group should announce their structure before they perform so the rest of the village can follow knowingly.

11. Ask the rest of the village to respond to each group's structure. What was clear? What was unclear? As always, Village Rules apply during feedback sessions. Why might one structure work better than another? Encourage vocabulary and language that was shared with them during story structure examples.

12. After all of the groups have shared and received village feedback, refocus on the village's observations and feedback. What do they **feel**? What do their **guts** say?

Step 2: Adding Layers

13. Send the village back to their collaborative groups. Ask them to discuss the feedback, what worked and what did not. Give them some time to 'fix' the unclear issues—they should be doing this 'fixing' physically.

14. Tell the groups that for this next round of collaborative work they will add the following elements to their structure stories: Illustrate clearly a *Who, Where* and *Why* in their stories. These need to be examples, not the entirety of each element—i.e., not every character, not every setting.

15. To help support these new elements, allow the groups to use one-word dialogues—where characters can speak one word at a time.

Exercise/Game:
One Word Improvisation

- Clap the village into a circle. Ask for two volunteers to come to the middle of the circle. Using Freeze Improv as the foundation, the actors can use one-word at a time to assist in pursuing their objectives.

- To kickstart the game, ask the village to supply the *Who, Where, Why* of this initial scene.

- Ask the two actors in the middle to engage in the scene using one-word at a time, when needed. Only use a word when needed, not to just have a word. Do not allow the words to diminish the physical commitment.

- When villagers on the outside of the circle see an opportunity to change the Who, Where, Why of the scene they can yell 'FREEZE,' which freezes the actors in whatever position they were in, the villager that yelled 'FREEZE' comes to the middle of the circle, taps the actors they'd like to replace, that actor retreats to the outside of the circle, and the new scene commences with new *Who, Where, Why*.

- Use this exercise/game to physically illustrate the use of one-word dialogue. Be aware of the difference between those scenes when one-word is used naturally, thus truthfully, and those scenes when one word seems forced, thus reading false.

- Once the lessons of **One Word Improvisation** have been learned through action, return to the collaborative group process as you develop the structure of your story with your students.
  Picking up...

16. Send the village back to their structure collaborative groups. Remind them of the new additions: A) Illustrate clearly a *Who, Where* and *Why* in their stories. These need to be examples, not the entirety of each element—i.e. not every character, not every setting. B) To help support these new elements, allow the groups to use one-word dialogues—where characters can speak one word at a time.

The previous exercise, One Word Improvisation, should have provided a helpful model. (15 minutes)

17. As you move about the room be on alert for students making this more difficult than it is. Its not 'starting over again,' it is taking what worked best, fixing what did not work best, and adding layers of clarity so that we can achieve our primary objective of this collaborative session: To identify and choose the structure (*Who, Where, Why*) that serves our story best. There is no competition between groups—the village is working for the village. Allow each group to find its way through the process. Struggle is underrated—ease is overrated.

18. For the overachieving groups who are 'done' early, challenge them to add additional layers of *Who, Where, Why* to their stories. There is no such thing as too much preparation.

19. Each group shares their physical structure story with the village—each group should announce their structure before they perform so the rest of the village can follow knowingly.

20. Ask the rest of the village to respond to each group's structure. What was clear? What was unclear? Why might one structure work better than another? How did the additional elements (*Who, where, Why* and One-Word dialogue) illuminate or dilute

21. After all the groups have shared and received village feedback, refocus on the village's observations and feedback. What do they **feel**? What do their **guts** say? Which structure seems best for our story?

22. Village Heartstorming: Choose the final structure for your story. The village has spoken.

23. Remind the village of the structure they chose by sharing the image shown previously. Ask a student to verbally review the central elements of the chosen structure (i.e., Climactic) while the rest of the village visually follows and contributes: Stasis, Inciting Incident, MDQ, etc.

Step 3:

24. Ask the village which segment of the story structure (Rising Action, Return to Stasis, etc.) they have immediate ideas for and connections too. Direct them to split into these groups. Make sure each segment of the structure is represented.

Assignment:

Collaborative Homework

- Each group is to meet outside of class and collaborate to write (build) an outline of their structure segment of the story.

- Be as specific as possible-liberally choose character names, locations, etc.

- Be as imaginative as possible—the power of abstraction

- Think BIG, as though there is an unlimited budget!

- Don't worry about neatly fitting one segment to the next, that won't happen. We will address transitions from one segment to another later.

- As a village we will decide which ideas and elements we will keep and which we will respectfully omit.

- Play with dialogue –they can continue one-word sentences.

- Upon returning to class each group will present their work to the village.

- They will first share their work verbally.\

- They will then share their work physically by staging their ideas using the rest of the villagers. (i.e., you're a calm tree over here, you're an angry mountain here)

- Be **bold and brave** with your choices—imagine each detail is 100% correct!

- You must have fun. If you stop having fun, you are doing it wrong.

Releasing the village to the world of homework is a symbol of trust and an excellent way to test the power of your community. Each group is charged with extending the village to a new environment (at least new for practicing the village rules) where the same expectations exist—each hero moving from the *known* to the *unknown* armed with the tools of the village to protect them from the dragons out there (scheduling conflicts, inadequate meeting locations, etc.). Who would've thought the village was mobile?! This is the first step to, perhaps, the greatest possible outcome of AFP's story-building process: Using the unique tools of *community building, conflict resolution* and *identity exploration* to create new villages to build new stories. Those are lofty expectations for their first homework assignment—I'm just reminding you of the ultimate goal. In the meantime, send the students off with clear **objectives**, strong **structure,** and sharp **clarity** as they continue to build their story within their collaborative groups. We will welcome these groups back to the village with their structure story work in the next section of the book, **Act IV: Sharing the Story.**

#Breadcrumb Alert#

The Dovetail Effect

While working on one section of the story-building process, it is natural and expected that you automatically (albeit subconsciously) begin working on the section ahead as you finish the section you're presently on. This is an organic occurrence and totally expected, as the elements collaborate like the villagers collaborate. None of this can happen within a silo or vacuum, these elements are interdependent on each other...they need each other and must coexist. So as the village is surfacing their story's theme, they will naturally be exploring structure—it's impossible not to. While they are exploring and 'trying on' various structures they are, by necessity, exploring the style of their story's delivery. This leaking from one stage of the process to the other is a 'wiggle effect' of its own; the next stage reveals itself when the story is ready for it as a result of the work from the previous stage. Thus, the structure of the story wiggles its way into the process at the tail end of surfacing the theme and the style of the story wiggles its way into the process at the tail end of the defining the structure. The village will earn the transition from one section to the next with their work. Like a dove's tail, where one feather overlaps another, it is the same with the story building process.

Building a Story is like building a house—*Structure* is essential

"The lessons from the peace process are clear;
whatever life throws at us, our individual responses will be
all the stronger for working together and sharing the load."

Queen Elizabeth II

The Story Building Process
Act IV: Sharing the Story

W ell, well, well, here you and your village are, two-thirds of the way there. Let's take stock of the process and your accomplishments thus far:

- You have built your village

- You continue to define and refine your community by practicing your Village Rules

- Your students are invested in the circle warm-up and understand the routine

- You have established important rituals to engage your students

- Your village has defined the **Theme** of your story—*What* your story is about.

- Your village has defined the **Structure** of your story—the *Who*, *Where* and *Why* of your story.

- And lots more of course....

The village's accomplishments throughout the process are important and have tangible value. Your students need to hear you review the list of their accomplishments aloud. Due to the nature of our work (fun, physical, exploratory) it will be difficult for your students to identify the work as work. At this juncture they will often not remember the steps and details they engaged in as being the story to this stage. They will be amazed and proud by all that went into their story journeys thus far. Practically listing and announcing their accomplishments will make their work tangible and identifiable as academic work. They've worked hard and need to be reminded of that!

Now that you know the *theme* (What) and *structure* (Who, Where, Why) of your story, you now must turn the attention outward and decide *How* you will share your story with an audience. The third pillar of the story building process is the **Style**.

Style = 'How' You Share the Story with the Audience

It is helpful to think of your story's **structure** as the internal language of your story. This is an important roadmap for the village and will serve as the language and blueprint for your internal construction process. You will never advertise your story's structure. On the flip side, the story's **style** is the external language of your story, the way you deliver your story to the audience, the *How* you share your story publicly. *Structure* is private and internal; *style* is public and external. The village needs to incubate the story through trial and error, building and demolishing, until the appropriate structure is chosen. Then, and only then, will the village's story possess the integrity to support the *style*. You have heard the phrase 'all style and no substance' I am sure—the structure is the substance and we (the audience) want both. Last metaphor (for now): In the baking world you cannot present all frosting and no cake—the *structure* is the cake; the *style* is the frosting. Frosting is sweet and delicious, but unfulfilling without the cake. I belabor this point to make a point. *Style* is typically the first thing novice story builders think of when considering creating a performance. This is why most theater is of poor quality, especially when produced by people with no experience in building meaningful stories. Filled with positive intentions, I am sure, but devoid of the story-building knowledge you are acquiring right now. AFP's process attempts to eliminate the product driven thinking of the teacher, and the ego driven thinking of the student; end gaming like this will only lead to low quality results. Process, process, process! How do we maintain the disciplined adherence to the process? The power of the Village Rules speaks again.

The choice of style must be justified by **what's best for the story.** You must beware of the "cool factor" you will be up against with the student village. Like bees to honey, your students will be attracted to styles based on what seems coolest to them. A rock musical style will provide immediate connections for your students, but is it the best way to share your story? For *The Rock Horror Picture Show* it was the best choice for sure! For your story about inclusion or peer pressure...Maybe not. Like our exploration of structure, the choice of style is not merely a vehicle for you to share your story, it is *part* of your story. Choosing the correct style is as intrinsic to your story as choosing dialogue. It is helpful to think of style as another building block of the story itself rather than a fancy coat to put on your story. Whatever you can do and say to your students to drive this point home is appropriate. Your job is to expose your students to multiple style options and examine the why behind those choices aloud, in AFP heart storming fashion. Like so many elements of story building, things tend to look much different on paper than in action—when things are spoken aloud and physically explored story truth happens. As a reminder, in story building *truth* always outweighs *real*. There is nothing *real* about devising stories. We are creating magical truth that, we hope, will illuminate an important issue theatrically.

#Breadcrumb Alert#

As if your job as teacher, facilitator, director, and leader isn't difficult enough, you also have the important responsibility of filtering the many choices you put before your student village. A highly successful film director friend of mine once said her job was never to tell the actors, designers, and production team what to do. Rather, her job was "to simply open and close doors of possibility." That's your job too. Offering every possible story structure and style to your students will be overwhelming and ineffective. You must always be several steps ahead of the village in this respect. Only 'open the doors' to places you believe will help move the story forward and 'close those doors' that will take your students and story to places of confusion. Students, especially your brightest and most creative ones, will gravitate to new, exciting, and previously non-discussed options. While 'opening this door' may feel great for the student(s), it may derail the focus of your story and its needs. As a clever teacher you may have already guessed that this approach requires more research and preparatory work from you—yep, you're right!

Good teaching (like good parenting) is inconvenient. If your process for choosing the appropriate structure and style for your story is easy I would recommend reviewing what you've done up to that point— "ease" is not a positive sign. You are teaching, amongst so many other important life lessons, the value of resilience and hard work. I tell my students all the time: "Struggle is undervalued" and "Work is good." These are two philosophies that may be difficult to find on their smart phones but easy to find in life. Only bring structure and style choices to the village that you believe will inform the story, illuminate your lesson(s) and be effectively produced by your village.

If you don't have singers don't do a musical! This alert may sound contrary to the assumed equality of the village. You may have assumed, based on the village rules and our emphasis on treating each other well, that the village is a Democracy. The AFP story-building village is NOT a Democracy. There are moments where Democratic rules govern the process, but the students (villagers) never have the same influence or control over the process as the teacher (director). You must know more than the students for the story to be built—in fact, your students are counting on you knowing more. This is a non-traditional academic process that will feel unfamiliar to your students (and initially you). This lack of familiarity will result in insecurities without the strength and assurance of a leader. When mammals are insecure, they behave badly—they need direction, confidence, and stability. The idea that collaborative groups operate best when everyone has equal say is garbage; a myth perpetuated by people who live in a world of sitcoms and cartoons. Woodstock may have been a wonderful experience and loads of fun, but it certainly wasn't the format for sustainable learning. Those who attended (and can remember) will confirm this reality. You have the responsibility to lead the village to a place of success. Open those style option doors that you see as real possibilities to advance your story, and close those doors that will not. You will be closing far more doors than opening. In the end, students will come and go, and you will be left representing your stories at your school or organization. Your strong leadership is vital in developing your long-term reputation as a gifted story builder, educator, and activist.

Typical *style* examples are musical theater, puppetry, and dance. *Styles* can also include the many 'isms' of the arts, for instance expressionism, realism, and absurdism. There is no single style you and the village are searching for. The final *style* can be (and often is) a combination of *styles*, or a brand-new style unto itself. What's important about your eventual *style* of delivery is:

- The **clarity** of the performance rules your *style* dictates (i.e., singing when emotions are high).

- The **consistency** with which those rules are adhered too.

- The **commitment** to the execution of those rules.

"What *style* is best for the effective, entertaining, and educational delivery of the story?" must prevail as the guiding question. I will share some style options a bit later in this section after we return to the physical exploration—Body first, brain follows.

Let's re-connect with your village from where we left them at the conclusion of the previous chapter—this will give us a tangible application model for the transition into the *style* process.

Your village has been separated into collaborative work groups who are now returning from their homework assignment—each group has created an outline for their segment of the chosen story structure using one-word dialogues if necessary.

Picking up...

25. Ask the village about their collaborative homework experiences. What went well? What did not go well? What problems were solved? What problems remain? Ask lots of questions, allow other villagers to offer answers before you do.

26. During this discussion look for the 'wiggle effect' happening earlier than in previous discussions—less talk, more doing is an excellent sign.

27. Ask the groups if they require some collaborative time to finalize their plans for their presentations. They will

enthusiastically agree and accept this gift. Be on the lookout for groups that failed to meet outside for their homework and are attempting to use this time to 'fake' their presentation. Keep the time brief and be nosey. (5-10 minutes)

28. Clap the village back together. Establish a presentation order based on the structure (i.e., Stasis, Inciting Incident, Rising Action, etc.) (Re)Define the objectives, structure, and clarity of the assignment in your own words. These are not 'shows' they are physical expressions of the chosen story structure. Move the story-building forward.

29. Remind the village of their responsibility to physically participate in each other's structure segments and respond to what they see and feel. It is best to frame the responses with 'What was clear/unclear?' vs. 'What was good/bad?'

30. Allow each group to select a primary presenter who will read the outline to the village first, then (possibly another group member) lead the village through the physical staging of their structure segment. Reading first, doing second is important.

31. Move through each group's presentation. Allow each group to illustrate their ideas from start to finish without interruption—it's their time.

As you and your village move through this presentation process—this sharing of the collaborative work—be prepared for a noisy experience. The primary presenter who is leading the village through the staging process has full control and power. Your job as teacher is to remind and refocus the rest of the village when the energy spreads beyond the task (objective) at hand. Noise and fun are essential and expected. The primary presenter is the 'director' of the scene—it is important for the rest of the village to respect this role. When a village member is asked to play the 'river' or the 'lion,' they are expected to do so immediately and fully committed. It is the primary presenter's responsibility to use appropriate and clear language to optimize the success of the exercise. Asking questions is a great default position for any director: "Lisa, will you be our scared, cold mountain stage left?" "Michael, will you please jump up and down upstage center to represent the rain?" Questions and adjectives always help. As I have mentioned, while we are invested in a process that will fluctuate and change based on the needs of each village, adherence to formal theater vocabulary is important as it suggests consistent high standards; There can be no freedom without discipline.

#Breadcrumb Alert#

Stage Directions

The universal vocabulary for stage directions is based on the proscenium stage (audience on one side facing the stage—most likely your high school auditorium was a proscenium stage), with the actors facing the audience. So, stage right is the right side of the stage from the actor's perspective facing the audience—stage right, is audience left. Stage left is the left side of the stage from the actor's perspective facing the audience—stage left is audience right. Upstage is the area of the stage furthest away from the audience, and downstage is the area of the stage closest to the audience. This vocabulary has historical significance, as early proscenium stages were raked (angled like a ramp) to assist audience sight lines. The highest point of the stage was furthest from the audience and the lowest point of the stage was closest to the audience, thus the actors had to walk 'upstage' and 'downstage' when moving about the set. Actors needed strong ankles and props could never be round! It is important to use these terms when blocking (moving) your actors and when the students are blocking each other about the stage.

Note: These stage directions hold true even when an actor turns her back to the audience—stage right, left, up, down are always based on the actors facing the audience. Center stage is smack in the middle of the stagearea—where every student wants to be!

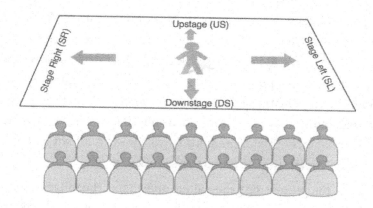

As the village moves each other about the stage to best illustrate their story structure ideas, many discoveries will be made. What worked well on paper may not work so well physically and vice-versa. Putting ideas (theories) to action provides a marvelous truth serum—you and the village will know immediately what works and what does not. Remind the village that when you immediately discard an idea that it's **good** for the process; it is as important to know what we *don't* want as it is to know what we *do* want. You will never know this unless you have ideas to throw away. We always build 10-15 stories every time we engage in the process—we can only keep one. The story scraps that we discard can be picked up and used for future stories. A wonderfully theatrical, exciting idea surfaced many years ago as I was building a story with the current student village. Every student wanted to include this element because it was so wonderful. We eventually realized that this idea was wonderful but, in the end, would not assist the current story—we had to let it go. Three years, several villages and over 60 students later the idea resurfaced and was used effectively in another story. The village is always growing and even though a current villager may never physically meet a villager from the past, they are always in perpetual collaboration—this singular village idea always provides comfort and confidence for our students. As you move through the structure stories realize that one group's ideas will spark another's ideas—allow these discussions to happen. As each group moves through their story, allow for the entirety of that group's work to be shared before making additions or omissions. Ideas physically shared will excite other villagers—this excitement is welcomed and can be shared upon the completion of the group's work.

As the presenting group alters and adapts the villagers acting in their stories ('Could your bird be angrier?', 'Can you make the giant larger and nosier?') they are, subliminally, investing in the *style* of your story. They are being particular as to *how* the story is being shared. Encourage your students to use multiple adjectives as they clarify the details of what they want. Remind them of their strengths within the circle warm up games and exercises—full commitment is essential, regardless of style. If there is a performance style AFP is known for, it is full-bodied, fiercely committed, abstract expressionism. The multiple adjectives will inform the work of each group.

Full Commitment is necessary at every step
of the story building process

Be aware of repeated adjectives, as these will be crucial as you develop the *style*. This repetition is the subliminal voice of the village organically defining the *style* of the story. Your job as teacher (facilitator) is vital here:

To publicly identify the repeated ideas ('It sounds like you all really want the environment to be dark, scary and mysterious?')

To close the doors on ideas that stray from the village voice ('I love the laughing sun image Beth, but it sounds like the village is moving to a more serious environment.')

Let's proceed...

32. Ask the village to do some heart storming:

- How did seeing all the structure stories make them **feel**?

- How did seeing them all together justify structure choice?

- Which sequences of the structure were most effective? Least?

- Was the structure's relationship to the theme clear?

33. Record the heartstorming of the village on the board.

34. Continue heartstorming:

- What reoccurring ideas were present?

- What motifs, images and metaphors surfaced more than once?

- What adjectives were repeated?

- What locations were effective? Repeated?

35. Record heartstorming of the village on the board. Note commonalities, omit ideas that clearly don't belong and seem out of place—those are for another story. Reflecting on the *theme* and *structure* as your guides, which elements on the heartstorming board will contribute most directly to the village's story? Allow for robust discussion and debate. Vote on issues that have split the village—Democracy rules, village rules ensure respect...the village speaks.

36. Put all the remaining, 'greatest hits,' elements in three columns: *Feelings, Structure* and *Adjectives*. The *Feelings* refer to your first question about the village's general response to the structure stories—these will be how we want our audience to feel after witnessing the story. The *Structure* refers to those elements that fit well within the chosen story structure—these are our building blocks. The *Adjectives* refer to the sensory qualities of the world of the story (i.e., dark, scary, electric, fluffy, tense, bright, happy)—these describe the evolving *style* of your story.

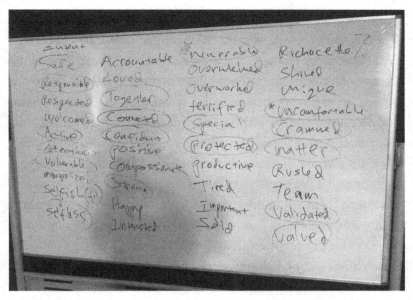

Greatest Hits on heartstorming boards are story building gold!

Conventions: Bring on the Magic!

Conventions are the magic of theater. These are the tricks we use to convey story elements to our audience. They can be physical: *Every time a character turns around in a complete circle, they age 10 years.* They can be part of the scenic detail: *Confetti coming out of the sky is rain.* They can be practical: *When an actor changes their hat they become a different character.* These are just a few examples—I am sure you have witnessed MANY. Regardless of the convention, they are crucial in creating the *style* of your story, emphasizing the magical capabilities of theater, and moving your story forward with economy and precision. One cleverly created convention can take the place of two (boring) pages of dialogue. The power of metaphors and symbols is evident in great stories. This is an excellent opportunity to activate your student's previous literary lessons in these areas *('…Involve me and I learn.')*.

With the work of AFP, we have become so enamored and dependent on the use of bold conventions, that it has become a trademark of our work. As our work has evolved, I have limited the number of physical props (canes, swords, books) from three to our present limitation: 0. Reason being, watching the school audience student's faces light up with amazement when they see my students *being* mountains, *being* bridges, *being* rain has been extremely rewarding. When these same students watched stories with actual mountains, bridges, and rain they were not impressed—how can you blame them? They are living in a world where the technology in film and television is at such a high level, current audiences expect these production values. But, when they see *people* making these things happen simply with their bodies, voices, and each other, they are spellbound. My theory behind this excitement is that they, the audience, become more invested in a story where they see themselves. It is difficult to imagine themselves as Matt Damon floating through outer space; it is easy for them to imagine themselves making their bodies into rain. Why is that easy? Because they've (you've) done it before—we call that childhood. This self-contained idea is also consistent with the ethos of AFP—you don't need lots of money and elaborate design elements to tell your story, you need **You**: your body, mind, voice, and spirit. This simple choice of limiting props and design elements has helped to define and redefine our mission with AFP. When students ask about which props can they have (and they always do), because they believe actual swords, fire and rain will be cool, I tell them the same thing: "You can have any prop you can imagine—you just have to make it with your bodies, voices, minds and spirits." It takes courage and discipline to personally create *conventions*. We are the Peace Corp of Theater, armed with our instruments, each other, and a story.

The students tend to worry about the believability of their *conventions*. They wonder if they will look silly or if their *conventions* will confuse rather than clarify. These thoughts come from fear of being seen (it's quite vulnerable to be a mountain in front of 200 strangers!) and not trusting the audience. Here are some convention rules to follow to combat these obstacles:

1. **Clarity**: Work out every detail of what the body and voice are doing to create the convention. Allow the village ample time for these creations. This will be the language, the *style*, of your story, no need to rush. There is no such thing as too much detail.

2. **Consistency**: The audience will accept any convention if it is delivered with consistency. If one actor is moving their fingers for rain and another is not, the convention will not work. This dedication to consistency will provide beauty in the story sharing.

3. **Commitment**: There is no such thing as 99% commitment or 110% commitment, there is only 100% commitment—either you are, or you are not. Complete dedication to every detail of your conventions will ensure its effectiveness. All audiences will recognize partial commitment as an opportunity to disengage from investing in the story; If the actors aren't fully into it, why should the audience?!?

> ### #Breadcrumb Alert#
>
> *This crumb probably goes without saying, but I'm going to anyway—after all, repetition is good pedagogy. I am sure at this juncture of the book your bridges from the story building process to valuable life lessons are well constructed. But, take a moment and look at the three words discussed above regarding conventions:* **Clarity, Consistency** *and* **Commitment.** *In my over half century of life on this planet, it is a scary reality that authentic attention to these words is nearly non-existent. Regardless of the context, the application of these words is desperately lacking interpersonal communication, work ethic, writing, relationship building, marketing, etc. It is difficult to find an arena in life where these words (and their accompanying practices) are not useful. If we are indeed teaching our students' skills applicable to their lives as potentially successful citizens, then we must emphasize the practice, development and routine of words like* **Clarity, Consistency** *and* **Commitment.** *This is not 'extra,' it's authentic, intentional education without apology. Your job as their teacher is to publicly announce the life lesson bridges frequently throughout the story building process.*

Remember, one characteristic that separates great actors from good actors is *courage.* It takes courage to fully commit to things that seem outside of our everyday lives, outside our familiar comfort zones, anything that can be perceived as not normal (aka "weird"). Conventions are the magic of theater; they are the theatricality of the story delivery—they are definitely not normal. The audience will 'normalize' these elements when they are completely dedicated to by the actors—the courage to commit will encourage the audience to jump right in and accept the story rules before them. We call this the 'Willing Suspension of Disbelief.' This willingness is a subconscious deal between the actor (village) and the viewer (audience) consecrated by these unspoken words: 'As a witness to this story event, I agree to completely accept everything you put before me IF you, the actors, are completely dedicated and invested in every moment of the story. I willingly suspend my disbelief and believe what you put before me provided each element is clear, consistent, and committed. The moment you break this deal I will no longer invest in the story and disengage from the story event.' This deal is present at every story being shared publicly, every-where, with no exception. In my experience, I am consistently amazed and inspired by the desire of the audience to enter the world of make believe. This entrance to imaginative worlds of wonder is embraced because, once again, we are wired to do so. As children, what was the best part of a new appliance or piece of furniture delivered to your home? The box of course! We couldn't wait for that darn lamp or washing machine to get out of the way so we could have that precious box—so we could enter the world of make believe! What was the box? A spaceship, an ocean liner, a castle, a race car...anything but a box, right?!? When we were called to dinner we couldn't possibly be bothered—we were busy exploring Mars or fighting monsters—we were busy at play with our *convention*. Fast-forward to the audience's desire to play—we crave this wonderful world of imagination (cue Willy Wonka) because we've been there before, because we were designed to dive into the world of dreams. This is the obligation of your village. This is why your conventions (that will create your performance *style*) must be attended to with *clarity, consistency* and *commitment*. You didn't let your mom interrupt your Mars expeditions, don't allow your audiences to disengage from your story.

Style Examples

International Styles—It's Not Just About Us

The story building process can be an excellent vehicle for multicultural, international and diversity education. Growing up in the United States tends to fill us with misconceptions about the rest of the world. Due to our country's strong influence on global popular culture, it's easy for young Americans to imagine that the way we do things is the way the world does things; especially in regard to storytelling. Hollywood and Broadway are impressive machines that have made their mark, masterfully, in virtually every corner of the globe. The appetite for the American story formula is insatiable. JayZ, Beyonce and Eminem have created the story standard through music. Disney and Pixar have created the animated story standard. Hollywood, NetFlix and network television have created the story for the screen standard. Impressive? Absolutely. Conclusive? Not by a long shot. What about the other 7 Billion people in the world, how do they tell their stories? Aha! The answer is in multiple, magical, and thrilling ways that will entice your students, thrill their senses, touch their hearts and introduce them to multiple cultures around the globe. The fastest method to learn about another culture is through their storytelling styles. Michael J. Fox could have saved hours and hours of time in his *Back to the Future* films by simply going to the theater of each new destination. Story is and will always be the shorthand of culture. As you dive into the research of international storytelling the sheer volume of options available to you will undoubtedly overwhelm you; your job is not to share all of them, just the one's you feel would be best for your story and, more importantly, the ones you feel would be best the vehicles for the lesson(s) you are teaching.

I'm not suggesting that you must be an expert in every culture's storytelling style from around the world—that would be unrealistic. I have provided several strong resources in this area for you at the end of this book. My suggestion is to only expose your students to specific story cultures that directly inform your lesson. For social studies its simple: if you are in the midst of your China unit, sharing the Peking Opera would seem wise. If you are working on symbolism and metaphor in a literature class, surfacing west African storytelling would be ideal. The central point is that there is a *reason and history* behind every story sharing style in the world. The reason for athletic acrobatics in Peking Opera can be traced to the national importance of the competitive desires of the Chinese royalty governing during the 18th century. The reason for the intense use of symbolism in west African storytelling can be traced to the fact that most people were illiterate in that region (not lacking intelligence, lacking the skill to read and write) and cultural histories were handed to new generations through verbal stories around the campfire—grandma used her surroundings (mountains, wildlife, agriculture) as central characters in her performances to guarantee the lesson was learned.

As I work with teachers from all over the world, I am struck by the common ties that bind them and their work together. One of the reoccurring frustrations I hear is teacher's 'inability' to teach life values. This bucket of life lessons was historically left to the family and the church (temple, mosque, etc.) to teach. The separation of Church and State combined with the dissolving strength of the family and religious structures has caused the expectation of this teaching responsibility to be left in limbo. Whose job is it to teach right from wrong? Whose job is it to teach personal responsibility? Whose job is to teach compassion, generosity, good will and, the most requested value I experience: Empathy? If you call yourself a teacher, this is *your* responsibility. As you review the story building process thus far, you will note our road is populated with multiple value lesson stops on the way to story completion.

In fact, those stops are intentional and the real reason we are engaging in this unique process in the first place. To me, the most widely ignored value in our young people today is *Empathy*. Based on the requests I receive, I'm not alone in this observation. We know our students need to define and build their empathy skills if they are to navigate their complex, global, ultra-connected worlds with any degree of success. This world is really not about them individually it is about all of us collectively—*We Before Me*. There are many non-western cultures who practice the *We* much better than us. There is an expected period in our student's brain development where everything must in fact feature their three favorite subjects (Me, Myself, and I)—we call that neural revolution *adolescence*. While this period may seem like forever, it will in fact pass and they will remember the valuable lesson that there is no such thing as "them" and only a world filled with "us." Students will only recall this information if it was taught to them without hesitation and will full intention. Immersing your students in the multiple story styles from around the globe is an excellent vehicle for empathy education.

Empathy is not sympathy—this is a popular and divisive mistake.

> **Empathy (noun):** *The ability to understand and share the feelings of another.*

> **Sympathy (noun):** *Feelings of pity and sorrow for someone else's misfortune.*

That's a huge difference, right?!? Empathy places the observer in the shoes of another without judgment. Sympathy assumes the experience of the other from a judgment of distance and "less than." So, you see, while this may initially seem like a matter of semantics it is much more than that—we can either teach our students to connect to others by experiencing understanding or teach our students to disconnect from others by assuming and belittling. Empathizing is a step toward life success. Sympathizing is a step towards colonizing. Yes, it's that important. Choosing the story styles you share with your students is not just about the story you are creating—it is about an intentional lesson in empathy. For those of you who prefer hard data about humanity's undeniable connections and proof of *We Before Me* please research the work of the National Human Genome Research Institute. In short, our bodies have three billion genetic building blocks, or base pairs, that make us who we are. And of those three billion base pairs only a tiny amount are unique to us, making us about 99% genetically similar to the next human.

The potential for imbedded lessons within the style choices for performance are limitless. Professor Google can help you with your research; the video examples are delightful and will be genuinely appreciated by your students. One of my favorite experiences during this stage of the story building process is to watch my students watching these unique style options—their creative connections are tangible! In the meantime, here are some examples of style choices that may help to inform your facilitation of *How* your students will share their story.

Heightened Text: Style Through Language

Why do actors sing in musicals? Because they must! Not because the director told them to sing, or because the orchestra is playing the introduction, but because mere spoken words not enough to accurately express the emotional values of the moment...they MUST sing! Mere prose (paragraph form) is simply too loose, too informal to authentically represent the high emotional levels some moments require. This shift from spoken word to song belongs to a theater performance style referred to as "heightened text." This is appropriately termed as the language in the story experiences a "lift" from a basic, conversational, non-structured, free-flowing format to an elevated quality of communication, structure and, most importantly, meter; there are strict rules to metered language. Meter can be simply defined as rhythm and cadence. More interestingly for your students, meter should be defined as "emotional muscle."

The moment, scene, character, or entire play *needs* the heightened language to be shared effectively with the audience. Heightened text becomes a convention, the magic of your story. Besides the entertainment value of heightened text (audiences love to sing, tap, move with the action) this style provides shrewd economy for your story telling. Your students will undoubtedly over-write their play—this is wonderful for your village's learning process, rarely wonderful for your audience. You have heard the phrase 'a picture is worth a thousand words," the same for a section of lifted, condensed, metered text. In three minutes, a song can introduce two young lovers, follow them through adolescence and college witness their marriage and have three children by song's end...now that's magic! I dare say not just magic, but smart story building. We can't keep the audience in their seats for 10 years, but we can take them on a hyper speed life journey using heightened text and span decades within the tight confines of a short play. As theater strives to keep pace with contemporary audience's shortened, layered attention spans, performances are trimmed from the traditional three hours to an economical 90 minutes on Broadway. Since AFP's work in the schools is dictated by class periods, we must keep our stories under 40 minutes—this forces us to use conventions that provide compact performance styles—we need to pack a big punch in small package. Heightened text is a strong option as you look for ways to wedge big ideas into small places. While singing in a musical is the most obvious illustration of heightened text, there are several other examples where the text is lifted and structured to provide an appropriate language container for the emotional stakes at hand. I will provide three short examples here including singing in a musical, Shakespeare's iambic pentameter and poetry/rap.

Heightened Text: Song

The popular Broadway musical Miss Saigon provides a great example of the power of song in the duet *Sun and Moon*. Miss Saigon follows the story of Kim, a 17-year-old Vietnamese girl who is forced into prostitution during the final years of the Viet Nam war. She meets Chris, an American GI who wants to take her away from the hell that is war. They are deeply wounded by the war and deeply in love with each other. In a touching scene where she has spent the night with him he finds it difficult to explain his profound feelings for her. He knows he wants her to stop working at the bar and live with him. She knows she is feeling things she has never felt and is also searching for words to express her emotional state. They both *need* to sing (heightened text) and thankfully the orchestra begins to play the introduction to *Sun and Moon*. The music immediately shifts the emotional mood to a heightened place, the actors' spines lengthen, their emotional subtext grows and grows until Kim begins singing:

> *You are sunlight and I moon*
>
> *Joined by the gods of fortune*
>
> *Midnight and high noon*
>
> *Sharing the sky*
>
> *We have been blessed you and I*

Well, geez, that helped! In five short lines sung to a tender, beautiful melody, Kim has expertly expressed what mere free verse, what mere pedestrian words could not. She has also expanded the scope and scale of the feelings by using metaphors and symbols—two muscular tools in heightened language. Putting words to feelings using metaphors is an essential component of the Contemplative Learning philosophy as well as the obvious importance to language and literature teachers everywhere. The scope of Kim and Chris's love has escaped the dirty soil of war-torn Saigon and elevated to the pristine, eternal world of the solar system—they are no longer mere people, they are the sun and moon. Kim's introduction of song has provided structure for tongue-tied Chris who responds:

> *You are here like a mystery*
>
> *I'm from a world that's so*
>
> *Different from all that you are*
>
> *How in the light of one night*
>
> *Did we come so far*

While not as eloquent as Kim (that's intentional and appropriate for their characters, cultures, etc.), Chris manages to put words to his heart. He is baffled by what he is feeling and manages to replace his pre-song stammering and frustration with words and meaning. As the song grows so does their satisfaction with each other and their hope for their future together. This relationship development is best exemplified through song when characters sing together—suddenly and magically Kim and Chris sing the chorus together:

> *And we meet in the sky*

Just wonderful, right?! We could spend an entire chapter analyzing this, or many other well-written songs, to dissect their story values. For our purpose in this section, it's important to realize the power of song as a potential style to deliver your story. The musical is America's single greatest contribution to world theater; the combination of spoken text and sung, heightened text, was a departure from Opera and spoken plays—a new style that has proven its worth time and time again.

If the imagery of sun, moon and the sky remind you of another pair of 'star crossed lovers' you are prepped for another example heightened text from a guy who knew something about the use of language...

Heightened Text: Shakespeare

I really must practice great restraint during this section. Tombs of books have been written about Shakespeare. For our purposes I will limit our discussion to a brief explanation of his use of heightened text and share a quick example from Romeo and Juliet. I am using popular examples (*Miss Saigon, Romeo and Juliet*) to provide relatable examples. I am in no way assuming or suggesting your students will be creating Broadway musicals or Shakespeare's language—just sharing examples for you to share with your students to light the fire of heightened language.

If Shakespeare's language was music, his choice of meter (iambic pentameter) is the base line. Ten beats per line, five of them emphasized (strong), five of them deemphasized (weak) make up the structure. If you remove the base line to your favorite music, you will notice the impact of iambic pentameter. Your favorite song will lack its guts, its muscle, its drive. When today's young people are driving their cars with their rap or hop-hop music turned way up, what you hear and feel is the base line, the drive of the song. You may not even be able to decipher what the song is, but you know the style because you feel the base line in your bones. This is the same case with Shakespeare's verse (iambic pentameter). If properly performed, the verse will drive the emotion, the scene, the story. Shakespeare also wrote in prose (free verse) with no structure, no meter. So why would a character speak in verse vs. prose? For the same reasons Kim and Chris sing in Miss Saigon— because they *need* too. Shakespeare reserved the use of verse for his high-stationed characters (kings, queens, princes, princesses, etc.) and for those central characters who were experiencing heightened emotions. These characters *needed* the heightened text to either separate themselves from the commoners or to accurately express the intensity of emotions they were experiencing. When you extract the iambic pentameter from the text you will note that it mimics the meter we all share as human beings—the heartbeat:

ba-BA-ba-BA-ba-BA-ba-Ba-ba-BA

(weak-STRONG-weak-STRONG…)

That's right, your heartbeat is the baseline to Shakespeare's music. This was intentional. Truth be told, Shakespeare made many mistakes in his plays: historical dates, geography, people's names, and events have all suffered Shakespeare's inaccuracies. Where Shakespeare never made a mistake (never) is his analysis of the human condition. His use of iambic pentameter is a primary tool for his insight into our souls. The weak/strong emphasis in his verse as suggested above is a 'perfect' line of verse. This means the character's emotional barometer is even, steady and controlled. When the verse is 'imperfect' it may look like this:

BA-ba-ba-BA-ba-BA-BA-ba-ba-BA

This is not a mistake by Shakespeare! Rather, it is a direct reflection of the character's emotional state: uneven, chaotic, and out of control. Have you ever felt out of rhythm? Of course, you have—your verse is off too in those moments. What do you try to do when your verse is imperfect? That's right, fight to return to perfect verse! That's exactly what Shakespeare's character's do—they fight to return to a perfect line of verse. Brilliant! Shakespeare's use of meter is no literary exercise—it is his code to the actors playing the characters in his plays—he supplies the emotional roadmap, and the actor simply needs to follow his lead. Unfortunately, most English teachers do not teach iambic pentameter for this purpose and most actors deny the emotional directions during performance (huge audible sigh). Allow me to share an example that will reflect well on Kim and Chris and our discussion of heightened language.

In a play called *Romeo and Juliet*, our two teenagers don't spend much time together. Everyone talks about them, but their face time is extremely limited. Therefore, each precious moment must be tended to with care and precision. Shakespeare has taken care of that from their first conversation. This conversation occurs at Juliet's home during a great party her father (Capulet) is throwing. Romeo is of course a Montague, a family enemy to the Capulets. Romeo and Juliet have seen each other for the first time and need verse to convey the intensity of their beating hearts:

ROMEO

If I profane with my unworthiest hand This holy shrine, the gentle fine is this: My lips, two blushing pilgrims, ready stand To smooth that rough touch with a tender kiss.

JULIET

Good pilgrim, you do wrong your hand too much, Which mannerly devotion shows in this; For saints have hands that pilgrims' hands do touch, And palm to palm is holy palmers' kiss.

ROMEO

Have not saints lips, and holy palmers too?

JULIET

Ay, pilgrim, lips that they must use in prayer.

ROMEO

O, then, dear saint, let lips do what hands do; They pray, grant thou, lest faith turn to despair.

JULIET

Saints do not move, though grant for prayers' sake.

ROMEO

Then move not, while my prayer's effect I take. Thus from my lips, by yours, my sin is purged.

JULIET

Then have my lips the sin that they have took.

ROMEO

Sin from thy lips? O trespass sweetly urged! Give me my sin again.

JULIET

You kiss by the book.

Nurse

Madam, your mother craves a word with you.

Of the many amazing elements of this short, heightened text dialogue, perhaps the most significant is the fact that Romeo and Juliet create, unbeknownst to themselves, a sonnet together. The only thing more heightened than iambic pentameter in 'Shakespeareland' is the precious sonnet—this is the filet mignon of literature! Simply speaking a sonnet is:

- 14 lines long

- Lines 1-12, Rhyming scheme is every other line (1-3, 2-4, etc.)

- Lines 13-14 creating rhyming couplet

Shakespeare saved his sonnets for his diary. These 154 penetrating, personal explorations were reserved for his most intense longings, loves and frustrations. Historians suggest that he never meant for these to be published or shared publicly as they dealt with multiple indiscretions, secrets, and fantasies. Shakespeare's 37 plays were for us mere humans to feed upon, but his sonnets belonged to him. By the way, if you ever want something published just demand that is remain unpublished and when you die it will become published—Shakespeare teaches lessons he's not even aware of!

Back to our teenage lovers—how amazing it is that they create the highest form of language, a perfect sonnet, the first time they meet!?! This ultra-condensed elite language style is proof that they belong together. I tell my students all the time, if you meet someone new and create a sonnet with them, marry them! This is brilliant story telling; not only do Romeo and Juliet create literary perfection (word sex) at their first meeting, but they also spend the rest of the play trying to create more sonnets together (that's what hormonal teenagers do)! Unfortunately, this is the only sonnet they are allowed to complete as all future attempts are interrupted by other characters, actions, and problems. Thus, the central struggle and theme of the story is reflected and replicated through the textual style of the story. The audience feels the frustration of two beautiful, young people fighting to connect but with too many obstacles preventing it. They just want to make sonnets but cannot.... *What a tragedy*...exactly.

We could spend the rest of this book examining the metaphors and language sounds imbedded in this famous dialogue, but for now realize the powerful potential of heightened text as a style for your story. I never ask my students to 'write Shakespeare,' but they always ask me if they can use poetry, spoken word, hip-hop and rap. These literary forms are their Shakespeare—I love it. Using bold language has multiple uses for your village stories and can be a powerful style to deliver your performances. The question always must be: How will this choice illuminate the sharing of the story? *Miss Saigon, Romeo and Juliet* offer possibilities for you and your students to chew on.

Shakespeare's "Arden": Style Through Environment

Not only does Shakespeare provide a textual opportunity to explore style, but he also provides an ideal environment for the intensifying of style, in *Arden*. Specifically, Arden is the name of the forest the characters retreat to in his play As You Like It. During Shakespeare's time the forest of Arden was a once magical place known to Londoners that had lost its luster and was in a state of disrepair. Arden plays an important environmental role in As You Like It as the forest becomes a place of inversion, cross-dressing and unsettled gender roles. The escape from the court changes the characters and creates a space of sexual freedom and chaos, where women take control and men learn lessons in romance. This is not the only play Shakespeare uses this rule breaking retreat (*A Midsummer Night's Dream, Timon of Athens*, etc.) In the comedies, the forest becomes a distorted version of the court where social rules are broken, creating a sense of jovial confusion before a return to civilization in the final act. The use of such a literary environment is a smart and useful story building choice as characters tend to learn more in locations of fantasy where all things are possible—we must lift the constraints of society of our protagonist, so she is free to make crucial life discoveries. Alice must go to Wonderland, Dorothy must go to Oz, Harry must go to Hogwarts and Dr. Indiana Jones must travel to snake-filled pits in Nepal. These are their "Ardens," a place where all bets are off, social rules are broken and reality as we know it is turned upside down—a perfect place to learn! Surfacing the use of "Arden" with our students will provide a ticket to fantasy and creativity. It's no longer "weird" to express a convention (i.e., flying like an airplane), in fact its expected and would be weird not to in Arden. They know "Arden" because their video games are filled with "Ardens" as are their favorite movies and TV shows. The creation of your "Ardens" should be fun, imaginative and specific. These environments automatically call for enhanced theatricality, thus a greater and more intense use of your conventions. My students have created stories where the characters can only use heightened text in "Arden," only move in dance in "Arden" or only personify machines in "Arden"—the choices are unlimited in! Some rules to govern your "Ardens" are:

- Social rules of stasis must be broken

- Physical and vocal actions must be enhanced and exaggerated

- Protagonist(s) must meet multiple learning opportunities

- Protagonist(s) must enter Arden from stasis and return to stasis after lessons

- The bigger and more extreme the choices, the better

- "What if _____?" is a great prompt

Young people love to create "Ardens" as it is their dream come true: Craft a world where all of the silly adult rules don't exist and our rules govern the land! (i.e. the only food available is candy, cake and ice cream). The environment of "Arden" is fully reflected in the dramatic structure the Hero's Journey as the "unknown," thus there will be many forces in stasis warning your protagonists of the dangers lying ahead, but you know there will be mentors and helpers to provide a glossary for the rules in your "Arden." You will note, now that we've consciously surfaced this routinely used storytelling environment, its impact on many stories. "Arden" is a special place in story building, and I encourage you to explore its use with your student villages.

Some bold environmental style examples from past productions I had the pleasure of directing at Buffalo State follow...

Antigone by Sophocles: Post Apocalyptic

Julius Caesar by Shakespeare:
Women Conspirators, High-Tech

The Space Between (AFP): Abstract Expressionism

Dance: Style Through Movement

Remember, a central goal of Story-Based Learning is to move the content of the lesson from the head (mind) to the soul (heart) of the student. The bridge for this transition is the body. Students love to move, especially when they are trapped in their desk prisons for most of the day. I am often shocked by the physical shyness of my students in class, but when I see them by chance off campus in a club or other popular night spot in Buffalo, they are dancing like professionals! Students have been told to "behave" for so many years that they believe moving is misbehaving, especially when it involves dancing to their favorite music. Tapping into your student's love for dance can be a huge benefit to your story building.

Here's a fact to move you along: We are no longer an "audience." This word was based on a group (Old French, Latin) of spectators gathered to hear (audio) a performance, speech, or other public sharing of information. During the Renaissance, there are diaries of Elizabethans who wrote entire scenes from plays without mistakes two weeks after they witnessed the event! Their audio perceptions were finely tuned and not interrupted by the multi-sensory world we now live in. We no longer listen to theater, music, or speeches...we see them. "Have you seen Lady Gaga's latest song?" "Did you see Kanye's tweet?" We are a 'visience'. Us older folks can be as frustrated as we'd like about the departure of the good old days when we listened to our beloved classic rock albums in our rooms for hours. Our students SEE everything in ways we never did—they are expert visualizers. A three-minute video of Beyonce's latest song does all the story telling they need—concise, exciting, and highly produced. It's no wonder traditional theater is battling to attract young audiences—they must compete with amazing visual story sharing. Since it's in their vocabulary, why not allow your students to create physical visual language for their story style? When you ask them to share examples of dance as style, they will invariably share styles reflected in their current music cultures (hip-hop, rave, rap, clubbing, etc.). This is an opportunity to share other dance styles they may not be aware of: Ballet, Jazz, Tap, Ballroom and less formal dance structures like abstract expressionism, industrial and interpretive improvisation. Again, only open those doors to our student you believe will lead them to a place that will support both your story and your lesson. Pictures speak a thousand words so you will realize the more physical style choices you make, the less spoken dialogue you will need. The style of your story delivery IS a form of dialogue. Dance and movement are richly symbolic. If ten students were standing still with their hands stretching to the sky, their eyes wide open and mouths tightly closed, the audience ('visience') would interpret this as symbolic language and immediately activate their story making brains. Your job is, with your village, to manipulate and control what they are communicating through their bodies. This is the primary job of a choreographer. Utilize the format of breaking the village into small collaborative groups, give them a physical assignment (What does a terrified city look like using only your bodies?), and they will return with the makings of your physical language for the story—style heaven. After each groups shares their work with the while village continue to send them back with additional directions (How can you connect your bodies and represent the city as a group rather than individuals?) until you begin to form a cohesive style. Again, Arden will be an exceptional opportunity to expand these physical choices to new, intensified levels. This is fun, physical, exploratory work so make sure to remind your students that you are searching for the physical language to best share your story, not the most fun or cool dance moves.

AFP Students incorporate dance as their style choice

Puppetry: Style Through Another

"My puppets can say what my people cannot." These were the words of a master puppeteer I met in Myanmar (Burma). He was delivering a day-long workshop in traditional Burmese Marionette Puppetry to my students and I. My students were amazed by the detail, the tradition, the craftsmanship and the heart that went into each individual puppet. My students were completely blown away by his political commentary "My puppets can say what my people cannot." To a college student born in the U.S., puppets were for children and almost all of them lived on Sesame Street. The idea that these miniature mammals had something serious to offer the world was surprise to say the least. The truth is, puppets have been a major part of world story telling for thousands of years. My Burmese friend was a fifth-generation puppet master. This family tradition was not an expression of lineage in the Burmese entertainment industry, it was a cultural commitment to preserving stories vital to the survival of the Burmese people. Burma has a long history of being led by an oppressive government. This political reality is illustrated by the mass influx of Burmese refugees in the U.S. Buffalo New York is proud to be home to thousands of Burmese refugees. While my students who were traveling with me in Yangon (Burma's capital city) were intensely curious about the current regime there was little information available to reflect the difficulties of Burmese citizens. This makes sense as the government controls the flow of information to the public—why would they publicize their oppressive actions? My students found the answers they were looking for during the puppet workshop. Each puppet master we met could carve each character from a block of wood by memory. Each clothing designer could hand sew the traditional costumes the puppets wore because that's what her mother and grandmother taught her. The specific list of puppet characters and their stories were unchangeable. This underground storytelling has survived thousands of years because it had to—the need for cultural preservation exceeded the need for entertainment. The government could not imprison a puppet! Although there are many stories of puppet theaters mysteriously burning down and puppet masters disappearing in the night. Despite these very real and dangerous obstacles, the art of Burmese puppetry has survived. Despite the very real and dangerous actions of the Burmese government, the Burmese culture has survived.

Burmese Marionette Puppetry in Yangon, Burma (Myanmar)

"Puppetry itself is a complicated field that combines performance and technical skill with craftsmanship and humor," says master U.S. puppeteer and puppet maker Bob Flanagan. Flanagan worked with Jim Henson during the modern glory days of puppeteering with the Muppets. "A puppet's movements are a kind of expressive shorthand," he said, "even the slightest hand gesture, or a tilt of the head can speak volumes that actors or lines can't always get across." We relate more readily to a puppet and his experience because of the fictional layer between the puppet and the audience. We willingly suspend out disbelief ("That's just fluffy fabric being controlled by a person!") if this convention is attended to with clarity, consistency, and commitment. This requires great skill and training. In Burmese Puppetry the masters are in plain view of the audience as they artistically manipulate the strings of each marionette. Our focus moves from the manipulator to the puppet as does the focus of the puppeteer herself; The puppet and puppeteer become one. This is a powerful phenomenon of puppetry. This spiritual connection may be an important consideration for you and your students as you consider the style of your story.

Perhaps nowhere in recent history is the power of puppetry on greater display than in Disney's Broadway musical The Lion King. Not one but several world puppet traditions are utilized expertly throughout the delivery of Simba's classic story of becoming king. In a stroke of brilliance, Disney chose Julie Taymor to lead this animated film's transition to the stage. Taymor directed and designed the production—she had full control of the play's world (costume, set, lights, sound, movement, etc.) which is rare in professional theater. Taymor's deep connection to Asia surfaced the use of Japanese Bunraku puppetry, martial arts and Kabuki traditions. The result was an immensely diverse collage of bold theatrical choices from all over the world to create unique truth on stage—this approach is a central message in the play. As you and your students watch video clips from the show you will marvel at the power of puppetry—a power human actors could not create on their own. The need for puppetry is on full display in The Lion King (scan code below).

You do not need Taymor or her budget (over $30 million) to create vivid puppetry in your stories. Once the principals and philosophies of puppetry are shared and learned, the budget conscious choices abound. I have witnessed gorgeous and powerful puppet choices from student groups using socks, paper bags and shadows. These eloquent choices have benefitted from their simplicity. Socks, bags and shadows all have their histories in global storytelling—your students did not invent these ideas at their sleepovers or camping trips. Puppetry is a universal truth in their lives too—Sesame Street is one place to find puppet power, but there are many other places to explore as well.

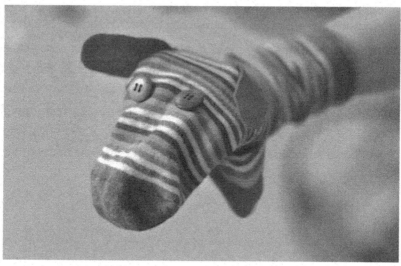

The Village Gifts: Style Right in Front of You

As you remember from **Act I: Building the Village** your village was bestowed with multiple gifts from your students. The once secret talents of your students were exposed in the sacred center of the circle to the delight of all (hopefully). As you were building your village, this exercise was important in creating trust, identity, and perspective. Your students learned new things about each other, and you had a chance to see some of your traditionally less successful students excel and shine.

#Breadcrumb Alert#

In general, providing kinesthetic and active learning opportunities for your students will flip the success curve in your classes. Those students who thrive in the traditional learning environment are easy to identify. Those students whose gifts lie a few layers below the surface are often more difficult to discover. Oh, how I wish we had the time to discover how each individual student best learns and create a curriculum tailor made for their successful learning. Impractical I know, but an educator can dream right? In the meantime, beware of the powerful impact activating your lessons might have on students who might otherwise be identified as 'struggling' or 'falling below' expectations. Specifically, the process of story building always surfaces and celebrates the gifts of the non-traditional learner. I am consistently amazed how the 'bad kid' is a hero and a model in our work. When we visit new schools, I am regularly warned by teachers and administrators of their 'problem students.' What was initially frustrating to me has become appreciated—they have highlighted the leader for me. There are no 'problem students,' just insufficient learning models provided for them in schools and, more importantly, rarely addressed in teacher training. What may work in an exam on paper rarely works for the student in the classroom. We must get the teacher candidates out of their seats and into their bodies as they explore multiple teaching and learning styles for their future students. Every child is really one creative teacher away from discovering his/her gifts. Story building provides an economical and rewarding mechanism for mining these gifts. Bring on the 'problem students!'

As you resurface the personal gifts from your students, see the literal impact their talents might have on the style of your story. Juggling, gymnastics, humming and knuckle cracking may all add meaningful content to your stories. The added benefits of including these gifts are that your students will be confident with the sharing and your audience will value the pure entertainment power of these choices. I learned to expose student gifts as part of the story building process by being surprised by their hidden talents late in rehearsals. I remember walking into the studio before a final rehearsal and witnessing one of my students executing standing back flips—one after another! I asked her "How long have you been able to do that!?" to which she replied "Since I was a little kid—I used to be a competitive gymnast." I wish I would have known earlier as the story could have used some back flips. Students will often separate their outside talents from their classroom personas. Sharing the gifts will allow for both symbolic (identity, confidence, perspective) and practical (direct style inclusion into story) applications in the story building process.

You see, the style of your story is an integral part of the story. Like the theme and structure, the style is another important thread in the fabric of your story. This is an important metaphor to consider because it so aptly represents the story building process. Every element of the process IS the story. Each thread touches, overlaps, intertwines and blends with the others. This connectedness is essential and important to the fabric of your story. Not only can theme, structure and style bump into each other...they must! The interdependence of each story element reflects the interdependence of member of the village. The story is a living tribute to your Village Rules...it is the result of activating these rules. As your students laugh, sweat, start, stop, sing, yell, hug, repel, dance, roll, whisper, hum, stifle and expand with each other, so will the building blocks of your story. Style is the opportunity to celebrate, share and parade your student's process for the public.

The Village Speaks: Selecting the Style of the Story

As you and your students sample the multiple style options for your story you have weighed the pros and cons of each choice. The central question remains your guiding light: *Which style is the best way to share our story with the public?* Keep things simple as you review the options with your students. By this time, you will already have a sense of which style(s) they have responded to favorably and which they have no time for.

1. Gather the village and let them know it's time to select the style of their story.

2. Ask the students for suggestions to consider as finalists. Put those suggestions on the board—all of the suggestions.

3. Open the possibility of combining styles to accommodate the story.

4. Remind the students of the power of their "Arden" in the play. The qualities of "Arden" will engage their willingness to be bold, creative and theatrical. How does the style of "Arden" compare to the style outside of "Arden" in the story?

5. Remind the students that the bigger their choices the better for the audience. Remind them we call shared stories "Plays" not "Seriouses," so have fun and play!

6. As you review each style choice on the board ask for student volunteers to advocate, justify, and explain why each style might work better than others. Encourage the students to use story-building language as they debate.

7. Narrow the choices down to two or three options. Open the village to a momentary Democracy: the students will vote for their style choice.

8. Record the votes on the board, majority wins, you have a style for your story, the Village has spoken.

Putting it on the Page: Stage Directions

NOTE: There are several free and easy script writing formatting applications available online. I recommend Celtx, RawScripts and Trelby. I encourage you to spend a day teaching your students (or them teaching you) how to use one of these applications. They will LOVE seeing their work looking professional, tangible, and real. This is an important milestone for the work as it becomes more permanent, concrete, and official.

If you are like the many teachers and students we have worked with over the years, you are wondering "When do we write the play?!" What you probably assumed was one of the first steps of story building is actually one of the last steps. That's not entirely true as you have been 'writing' your story from the get-go. Every moment you and your village have spent together has provided your library of content for your story—now just dump it on paper, right? Well, yeah, that's the easy way to communicate a challenging stage of the process. It is challenging because it will make permanent all of the creative exploration you and your village have been immersed in. It is challenging because of the connotation of writing that has been pounded into our psyches—the right and wrong, the sense of completion, the rigidity of the examination. It is also challenging because it requires making a choice to dive in and just do it! Initiating the writing process will require some teacher muscle for sure. You must become deaf to their groaning and moaning as you assign this step:

Collaborative Groups: Stage Directions

*NOTES: Have plenty of board space, hanging paper, etc. available to write on. This exercise will feel like the collaborative group structure exercise—that's intentional. The structure group work will work as a foundation for this exercise which will require additional details and choices informed by the chosen style of delivery.

1. Remind your students of their story-building journey thus far. Highlight the important milestones using Village Building, Theme, Structure, Style as your markers. Write these highlights for everyone to see, own and be proud of.

2. Resurface your heart storming products. Rehang your papers filled with adjectives, themes, ideas, quotations, phrases and feelings. This is the 'language' of your play.

3. Identify the elements omitted, common ideas, mutually agreed upon elements. Review their choices aloud. Allow students to do the writing on the boards—it's *their* story.

4. Remind the students that the Theme is your 'litmus test' to measure all of choices against—if the choice does not support the delivery of your Theme discard it and save it for another story.

5. Resurface the Structure the village has chosen. Review each stage of the structure (i.e. Stasis, Climax, Abyss, Return to Known).

6. Turn your teacher radar up: Be on the lookout for which students connect to which stage of the Structure.

7. Discuss Stage Directions, their purpose in a story and provide examples like this one from an AFP devised play **Hello, My Name is _____:**

> *ALEX wanders the forest curiously and hesitantly. As ALEX explores the forest, she passes by several trees played by the actors in the ensemble. Each tree swiftly and sneakily snaps*

in ALEX's face with voice and body and imme-
diately resumes their previous positions as
ALEX passes. ALEX makes her way back DSC
as ENSEMBLE swirls into two lines forming a
thicket of thorny bushes, also played by ensem-
ble, that ALEX has to push through and fight
off. In pain and scratched by the thorny bushes
ALEX makes her way through the haunting
and strange forest.

8. Explain to your students that action is far more interesting to audiences than words. Ask for a volunteer or two to verbally describe a setting using lots of adjectives and sensory (what does this place look, sound, feel, taste like?). Details and feelings are important ingredients in stage directions.

9. Looking at the chosen Structure, separate the story's journey into sections (i.e. Stasis, Introduction). Ask your students which structure section they most connect with. Separate the Village into working groups for each section (3-5 each depending on the size of your village).

10. Assignment: For homework, meet with your group and write the stage directions for your Structure section. When in doubt write more than less, use extra details, emphasize sensory...how does it feel in that segment of the story?

11. You will undoubtedly run into moments that require choices the village hasn't discussed yet (character names, locations, etc.)—use the library of heart storming sessions (take pics with phones) and make it up! By the way, we're making this whole thing up...keep going!!

12. Reminder: Every element of the story IS the story so be mindful of choices—every choice must be rooted in

the story as a vehicle to deliver your Theme. Example: Playwright Edward Albee's central characters in *Who's Afraid of Virginia Wolfe?* Are named "George" and "Martha" symbolizing America's "first couple" (George and Martha Washington) of divorce. Leave no stone unturned—everything matters.

When your students return to class have them present their stage directions in their groups by reading their work aloud to the village. The order of the presentations should coincide with the order of the story's structure (i.e., introduction group first, Inciting incident second, etc.). There should be a 'tag-team' effect from one group to another. You will note the student groups being inspired by the presenting groups—they will break into feverish whispers and intense scribbling as they hear other group's ideas that spark their own. Allow for this serendipity and give room for the creative eruptions. Channel their shared enthusiasm into the next steps of the work:

1. Allow your students to point out consistencies, repeated ideas and common denominators in their stage directions. What would they like to keep? What would they like to discard?

2. Surface the idea that the transitions between each structure section are, for good reason, unclear. They have been working in collaborative silos so its expected.

3. Ask the groups 'next' to each other in the sequence of the structure to combine for the next step of the work. (i.e. Introduction combine with Rising Action).

4. Ask the larger groups to meet, share their work with each other and create the transitions from one structure section to the next. (20 minutes)

5. Move around the room during this collaborative work session to encourage the use of village rules. The groups are larger now and will need to listen, take turns, etc.

6. Encourage each group to keep what's working and omit those elements that do not move the story forward.

7. Style will be a useful tool to use to activate the transitions between each section. What will the audience see, hear, feel?

8. Clap the village back together. Ask the groups to report their work to the village.

9. Embrace shared inspirations—give time to solidify choices (names of characters, locations, sequence of events, etc.)

10. Encourage final decision-making. Choose one or two students to collect the work from each group and compile the stage directions into one document that flows smoothly from one structure section to the next. Read aloud, this stage direction document should take the listener through the complete story from the beginning to end.

Collaborative Groups: Dialogue

It is important to note and remind your students that the one element that usually arises as THE most important element of writing a play is *dialogue*. The truth, as they are witnessing firsthand, is that the actual act of placing words on paper is the *last* part of the process. Another truth to share with the village: They have been *writing* the play from the onset—but perhaps not the way they imagined. Every moment together, every heart storming session, every conversation, every exercise, every game, every improvisation, every collaborative assignment, every vote, every debate, every photo, every current event, every poem, every prompt, every theme idea, every structure idea, every style idea...ALL add up to a library of language to be distilled, defined, and selected from as your students create the dialogue of the play.

If your students grumbled and complained about writing the stage directions (the action) of the play, they will typically raise the volume of their assumptive complaining when you introduce the dialogue writing stage. My suggestion: listen to their literary groaning, realize its based on a history of writing that may not be positive to them and probably has nothing to do with you and your class, and remind them how they have had false assumptions throughout this process that have proven untrue. They have everything they need to create meaningful dialogue for their play.

As you prepare for this stage makes sure you resurface all the saved artifacts of the process thus far and post them in your room in pain view of the village. This will impress your students as it will illustrate the sheer breadth of their work thus far—there will be LOTS of stuff hanging about the room. This should make your students feel proud of themselves and appreciate the volume of their work thus far. It is often difficult to remember everything that has gone into their process and, as you know, seeing is believing! This reality will be a positive jolt into the next stage of the work and their next assignment:

1. Return to your smaller collaborative structure groups where the students created the stage directions.

2. Using those stage directions, transitions, and sequences of action, write the dialogue for your story—imbed the dialogue WITHIN the stage direction scripts already created.

3. Dialogue is what the characters say, sing and sound throughout the story. By "sound" we mean sound effects that may be generated by the actors (wind, animal howl,

door creek, etc.). Share the basic definition and etymology of the word:

DEFINITION:

dialogue |'dīəˌläg, -ˌlôg| (also **dialog**) noun

-conversation between two or more people as a feature of a book, play, or movie: *the book consisted of a series of dialogues | passages of dialogue.*

-a discussion between two or more people or groups, esp. one directed toward exploration of a particular subject or resolution of a problem: *the U.S. would enter into a direct* **dialogue with** *Vietnam | interfaith dialogue.*

ORIGIN:

Middle English: from Old French *dialoge*, via Latin from Greek *dialogos*, from *dialegesthai* **'converse with,'** from *dia* **'through'** + *legein* **'speak.'**

4. Share an example of dialogue from a play script:

(From AFP devised play **Dear Me**. Reggie, a high school senior who is mourning the loss of his friend, is writing a letter to this friend when the spirit of Anne Frank appears.)

REGGIE

Woah, who are you?

ANNE FRANK

I am Anne Frank.

REGGIE

You're Anne Frank? That's not true, Anne Frank is dead! I learned about her in school and she died way long ago. Who are you? Is this some sick joke? Is someone messing with me? There is no way I am talking to a dead person right now!

(overlapping REGGIE)

ANNE FRANK

Sometimes people who have been dead can come back to visit the living because their stories got cut short.

REGGIE

So Charlie can come back and visit me? Could he explain why he killed himself?

ANNE FRANK

No, Charlie cannot come back; he chose to end his own story. But other people can come, people who you can learn great lessons from. You drew me here because of your words. You know, paper is more patient than people.

REGGIE

This is getting weird, Charlie used to say that. Paper is more patient than people that gave me the idea to write this letter to him.

ANNE FRANK

That's what I did when I was in hiding during the holocaust. I was so sick of being stuck in that annex all day long and I was so mad that the Jews were being targeting when we had done nothing wrong.

REGGIE

That's how I feel. I did nothing to deserve this and everything is so messed up. I feel so angry at everything.

ANNE FRANK

I reached the point where I hardly cared if I lived or died. The world was going to keep on turning without me and I couldn't do anything to change events.

REGGIE

I don't even care about school or my parents or friends anymore. Everyone and every little thing just pisses me off. I don't deserve this.

ANNE FRANK

That's what I felt. My mother drove me crazy and I was so angry at the Nazis. No one deserves to be targeted like that. No one should have to die.

Nazis surround Anne and take her away.

ANNE FRANK

Let go of me! People who struggle and suffer pain make much tougher and courageous soldiers than all you big mouthed freedom fighting heroes put together.

Anne Exits. Reggie remains on stage...alone.

5. Using a script creation application, ask each group to create the dialogue for their structure segments. Ask each group to communicate with the structure group next to them in the story to decide where one leaves off and the other takes over. They should be utilizing their transition collaborative work to accomplish this.

6. This can be assigned as homework or classwork. There is a tricky balance here: don't rush their work but also encourage them to jump into the writing using the materials posted around them. Starting the writing can be the hardest step, so encourage them to take a note from Nike and "Just Do It!"

My experience with thousands of students from middle to graduate school suggests that it is always difficult to begin the writing but once they do they find it easier than imagined. This is proof that their bodies know much more than their brains will suggest. Their bodies will remember all of the physical story building they have experienced and the words will pour onto the page. There is great irony about the assumptions of play writing. We once had a playwright at Buffalo State theater teaching, of all things, playwriting. She thought it hilarious and ironic that the course was listed as "writing intensive" by the college. As part of our general education requirements, each undergraduate student must take at least two writing intensive courses—these courses, you may have guessed, require more writing than typical courses. My colleague's thoughts, "That's crazy that playwriting is considered a 'writing intensive' course when the central focus of playwriting is to take words away not add them!"

7. Here's the point to share with your students: Actions are louder than words, so only use the words you and the characters need. We, as human beings, don't use full, grammatically correct sentencing when speaking with each other—less is best.

8. Require the students to read their dialogue aloud with each other before making final decisions. They are writing to be heard not read and will make obvious corrections once they hear how their dialogue sounds. They will write like

they talk which is excellent for the tone of your story as it is shared with other students. This authentic feel will be inescapable.

9. Tell your students they will return to the village to share their group's work with the rest of the village aloud. When they share their work they will have selected who will be reading which character with one person reading the stage directions.

10. As each group shares their work, invite feedback from the rest of the village (Village Rules apply). Send the groups back to collaborative time to make edits. Repeat this process until you have your Final Draft of your play. Congratulations.

This may seem like an abrupt ending to a lengthy process. I suppose it is if you compartmentalize each step of the story building journey, but you know better. Each small step of the process WAS writing the story, the play. You will be amazed at how smoothly (post assumption grumble) the writing segments of stage directions and dialogue go. This is not magic; it is the wonderfully satisfying product of the cumulative process you have dedicated the village too. They have been writing the play from the onset—you must always know this which is why you must keep every artifact from the process. You have filled your student's individual and communal tanks with so much story fuel that they will be relieved to put it all somewhere—you loaded them up for Story. You loaded them up for Life.

As your students gasp in amazement of what they have accomplished, remind them it was due to their hard work not some magic bestowed upon them by the story gods. Review the importance of establishing the village. Review the pillars of Theme, Structure and Style. Review the intentionality of the breathing rhythm of the entire process—the repeated movement of starting together as one, breaking away from the whole in small groups, returning to the village and repeating this rhythm throughout. Perhaps this might be a good time to review that Breadcrumb Alert from **Act II: Surfacing the Story...**

#Breadcrumb Alert#

There will be multiple times in the story building process where the village is separated into smaller groups, given a specific collaborative assignment and asked to return to the whole village to share what they have created together. These break out collaborations always have a time limit. The village sends small hunting parties out into the wild with an expectation they will return with gifts for the village. This separating, moving out in smaller pieces and returning to the whole demonstrates an important, intentional rhythm to story building. Clasp your hands together. Now, separate your hands and spread your fingers out wide as you move your hands away from each other. Bring your hands back together in the original clasp. Repeat this action several times. What does this rhythm remind you of? (Hint: Something your body does naturally thousands of times each day and it rhymes with Preathing) Breathing, you are correct! Story building is a natural human process like breathing. We ensure this important point by duplicating the breathing rhythm within the story building process.

Remind the village that certain stages of the story building process felt natural by design. Just like neuroscientists have discovered the brain's innate need for story to bring order to the chaos of our lives, so too have story builders around the world discovered that the innate rhythm of breathing will bring a natural fluidity to a complicated set of creative tasks. Building stories is essential and intrinsic to whom we are—it is an incredibly human thing to do.

Casting Your Story: Gacaca

Following the 1994 Rwanda Genocide there were thousands of perpetrators awaiting trials for their murderous crimes. Rwanda utilizes a western judicial system with judges, lawyers, juries, etc. If they had used the existing western system, it would have taken over 250 years to try the accused! In a stroke of brilliance, the Rwanda leadership resurfaced a pre-colonial judicial system indigenous to Rwanda called Gacaca (pronounced Ga-CHA-cha). Loosely translated, Gacaca means "justice on the grass" and was the code of reconciliation in villages across the country. Generally speaking, here's how it worked: Imagine you and I live next door to each other in a small, rural village. Amongst other possessions, we each own one goat. One morning you wake up and realize your goat is gone and there are two goats in my yard—one clearly yours. You ask me "Did you take my goat?" and I respond, "No, what are you talking about, of course not." We are at an impasse. Another neighbor witnesses our dispute and rings the bell signaling to the entire village: Gacaca time! Each member of the community is obligated to attend, and pre-selected elders will facilitate the proceedings. A long table faces the grassy hill where most of the village sits. Behind the table are the elders, the victim (you) and the accused perpetrator (me). Here are the mandatory elements for the Gacaca proceeds to play out:

1. The ultimate goals are communal understanding and reconciliation.

2. Complete honesty is expected from everyone—to be "Good of heart."

3. Any villager who knows something about the conflict MUST speak up.

4. If the perpetrator has been found to be guilty, they MUST publicly admit their wrongdoing and publicly apologize to the victim.

5. The victim MUST publicly forgive the perpetrator.

6. Under the counsel of the elders, the perpetrator and victim must create a reconciliation agreement.

7. Story (the health of the village) is First.

In our above scenario, imagine my guilt was exposed by a neighbor who saw me take your goat. I must confess my guilt with an explanation if appropriate ("My daughter was ill and needed more milk than my one goat could provide") to the entire village. You must, in turn, forgive me. We then, with the assistance of the elders, create a reconciliation plan together. You will have my goat for two weeks and I will help you build your new roof. We shake hands and drink some banana beer (not as delicious as it sounds) to seal the deal. The banana beer is there to make sure we leave the Gacaca smiling.

So, other than sharing a completely cool judicial alternative to western law, why would I share Gacaca with you now? As you already know, I believe wholeheartedly that the Rwanda post genocide recovery process should be shared with as many people as possible. Nearly 1,000,000 people were tried successfully by the Gacaca system—a system that gives the power of a nation to its people, not its policies. Rwandans were in charge of Rwandans. The future of their country, their new story was to be told by Rwandans; not colonists with ulterior motives, not governments imposing their will. As a dear Rwandan friend once told me "We are the ones who created the mess of the genocide—President

Kagame has given us tools to fix what has been broken." In the end, the themes of Gacaca are similar to our Village Rules:

Story is First (The story is the future of Rwanda)

We Before Me (We know we cannot do it alone)

These are ideal concepts to move into the casting stage of your story with. Was this too profound of a metaphor? Absolutely not! We have been unashamed about the story building process being a clever guise for multiple life lessons. Rwanda is a library of life lessons—I use them often.

The casting (who is playing which character in your story) of your play should follow the village ethos you have created thus far. Like every choice you have made along your journey, the casting choices should reflect:

What's the best choice for our Story?

We must put **We before Me**.

Gacaca Casting:

1. The class period before the actual casting, share the Gacaca model with your students (powerful videos available on YouTube). Tell them this process is the inspiration and model for how they will cast their play. Ask them to re-read their story at home and return to class with specific ideas for who should play who. Remind them: Every choice must go through the filter of *What's best for our story?*

2. When they return to class assemble the village into a circle, sitting down. Explain that it is highly unique for the actors to have a say in casting—in theater, the director usually makes these choices independently. As you re-emphasize the tone of the proceedings, be sure to clarify how much

time you have allotted for this process and that it is not a "popularity contest."

3. Explain that the village rules apply—the circle is sacred—this is a space of trust, listening and non-judgment. Every village member is safe to speak and share their thoughts.

4. Beginning with the protagonist(s), open the space for nominations; self-nominations are acceptable. Explanations and justifications must accompany all nominations. By taking turns, heart storm conversations about choices. When you feel that you have narrowed a particular character's casting options to 2-3 village members, ask the nominees if they accept the nomination. Once you have the 2-3 finalists for each role, open the village to a temporary Democracy: Everyone vote for your choice. You can vote eyes open or closed—I've done both and always let the students decide.

5. Repeat this process for each character.

6. Important: In every devised play I have ever facilitated the actors in the ensemble are, by far, the most involved people in the play. The ensemble is the environment (the ocean), the large props (the school bus) and the soundtrack (howling winds) of your story...the ensemble is BUSY. Do not allow those who did not receive named roles believe they are less important—quite the opposite.

7. Now that your play has been cast, conduct a read-thru of the script with the chosen actors playing their newly received roles. Demand that the ensemble actors voice their parts whenever possible (the crowd roared, the drums welcomed the guests, etc.). Ask the village to fully commit to their characters—nothing is gained from polite, quite read-throughs.

During the Gacaca Casting, you will note many interesting dynamics. There will be surprising consensus on who should play who in the play. Trust the village's instincts here. The students will be highly protective of their story—encourage this instinct and applaud their ownership. Compromise must happen and your students will be pretty good at it. There will undoubtedly be moments where two students are right for the same role. This conflict will create the village to consider what other characters they might be right for. I have directed many plays where the best possible choice for the lead did not end up playing that role because the actor who was my second choice could *only* play the lead while my first choice could play several roles. What was best for the story was to cast my second choice for the lead to free up my first choice for other roles. This issue will surface with your story building too and be sure to explain it clearly to the village. It is a great opportunity for you to model "Story First." The Gacaca casting process is a terrific vehicle to activate the village rules.

Gacaca Courts: Rwanda, 2007

Gacaca Casting Model: A Buffalo middle School, 2019

From Page to Stage: Rehearsing Your Story

The story is now ready to find its 'legs.' It's time to put your student's bodies *into* their stories so they can complete that important central nervous system cycle—they will now *own* their work by physically inhabiting their story. This section is the least Democratic section of the process. The students will not see themselves as they are on stage—you, their teacher now director, will maintain the audience perspective. The students want you tell them what to do at this juncture. There will be several opportunities for them to physically create elements of the story and you must be intentional about carving time out of the rehearsal schedule for that (i.e., "I need four of you to create a car with your bodies and three of you to be road signs.") The overall physical traffic of your story performance is called blocking. You must provide a plan for the movement of the characters in your story. This is not a theater directing book nor do I expect you to suddenly know how to move bodies around a stage artistically. If you have previous experience staging plays by all means use this experience. If you do not, don't worry. Here are some foundational rules to assist you as you begin to block your village's story:

- All movement must be the result of an actor's objective. Ask the actors "what do you want?" and allow that answer to dictate the blocking. Never allow actors to move without purpose or objectives.

- Provide an environment and its parameters ("The forest exists from here to there.") for each scene before you begin to block it. Actors must know where they are and what's in their way before moving. Bring in photos or drawings of each scene to show actors before blocking.

- Always speak to actors in theater terms: stage right, stage left, upstage, downstage, center stage, off stage.

- Remind the actors consistently of where the audience will be. Typically, that means proscenium style (audience all on one side like your traditional auditorium) which means they must 'cheat' their performances to the audience both physically and vocally. If it feels real it's wrong! "Up and out!" is something to say often.

- Identifying the audience as the performance target is both practically important (previous bullet) and philosophically important as well. The sharing of story is a *public service*—it's about the audience not the actors, the actors are merely vessels for the story. Acting, thus, is not the selfish exercise it is so widely perceived to be (that's *bad* acting), it is, rather, one of the most self*less* exercises imaginable. This is a rare opportunity to combat the teenage mentality, so tell your students often: "It's not about you."

- Practice the village rules when moving about the stage—generosity, sharing, listening, and allowing are great attributes to remind the actors of.

- Decide if the actors who are not in the scene are off stage or on stage in view of the audience but not engaged in the scene. Develop a convention for this (i.e., when actors turn their backs to the audience, they are not part of the scene.) I highly recommend keeping the entire village on stage at all times—this suggests the We at all times and creates a positive tension for the audience (what's happening next?). This strategy also alleviates unprofessional whispering backstage and provides a vehicle to show off the village's enhanced focus skills developed in the circle games.

- Bigger choices are better. Direct your students to be bold and silly with their bodies and voices. Self-doubt and self-consciousness will always diminish actor's choices—combat this early and often by directing your students to make big, brave choices and celebrate them when they do immediately.

- When at a creative fork in the road, revisit your theme and ask, "Which choice helps us to deliver our theme best?" The choice will be obvious.

- When students ask: "What should I be doing?" Return with the questions: "What does your character want (objective) right now?" and "What if this were you, what would you do?" Directing gold.

- Divide the sections of the play into clean, defined sections to be rehearsed. This may already be done in the writing (acts, scenes, etc.), but if not, you should always rehearse in naturally complete sections. For instance, don't stop in the middle of a scene—finish the scene. Doing less with clear sections is better than leaving rehearsal in the midst of unfinished sequences.

- Repetition is good pedagogy. Rehearse small sections at a time and always leave tome to review—let them 'run' the section without interruptions. This will give them (and their central nervous systems) an opportunity to learn the material in the way they will be sharing it. I always begin each rehearsal with a 'run' of the section we learned last rehearsal—engaging and ensuring muscle memory, trusting the brain will follow. These sections should grow until you have two halves, then eventually one whole section (aka: the show).

- Allow for heart storming sessions when confronting scenes, choices and options that are just not working. Be open and honest that this is not about one person but, as with everything else in the process, that this is about 'us' and 'our' story. We before Me.

- While directing is not a Democracy, carve out Democratic opportunities for the village to create elements of the story. For instance: You know there is a giant bus in a particular scene. Allow the village to collaboratively create this bus by improvising, discussing, and choosing the best way to make this happen. As you might have guessed, my preference is to frame these creative sessions by taking outside props out of the conversation and asking the village: "How can you make this bus with your bodies and voices together?" You will discover your student's creative brilliance I promise.

- The ultimate goal (Super Objective) of your direction is to give the play to your students. This ownership development starts with you talking, directing, and guiding while your students listen and apply. As the rehearsal process evolves you should talk, direct and guide less while your students should be adopting full control of the sharing of the story. Their complete ownership of the performance is vital for its eventual success. As their confidence and ownership increases, more responsibility should be given to them. They clearly 'get' the show now, so you can tryst them to make choices based on this 'getting.' The dialogue should now sound like: (student) "what should we do at this point of the play?" (you) "I don't know, it's your play, what do you think should happen?"

- Plays are problems. Producing plays for performance is larger problems. Your student village is now filled with problem solvers—you have trained them throughout the story building process—make them solve the problems. As they solve problems their pride of ownership will increase. They will eventually not need you at all—Teacher heaven!

- Rhythm is important. The energy and tempo of your story should coincide with your chosen structure. For instance, the pace and intensity of the action on stage should increase as the story moves through the rising action and reach a crescendo at the play's climax. Every actor I have ever directed will hear my voice long after the play is over, "Bigger, Faster, Louder!" By the way, I say the same three words to professional actors as well. Directing gold.

- If the play's tempo is dragging, have them do a speed-through, where everything is sped up—lines, movements, action is all moving 10 times faster than normal. It will feel so fast to the actors, just about right for you.

- Allow your chosen story structure to dictate the pace of the performance. No need to start from scratch—your structure is your pace guide. i.e., In the climactic structure the pace of the show should be steady and calm during the introduction until the inciting incident, then the pace should intensify up the rising action and consistently build in intensity until the climax. The pace should find a new clam as the story makes its way down the falling action and its return to stasis.

- Fight call. If there is any risky physical action in your play, conduct a preshow 'fight call' before each performance to move through the actions slowly and safely. Do the actions ¼ speed, then ½ speed, then ¾ speed then full speed. Safety, safety, safety.

- As you move through full runs of your show the 'performy' monster is bound to show up. This monster loves to be on stage and expresses this love through your students by overacting. This over-the-top acting feels great for the students doing it and terrible for everyone watching it. Bring your student actors back to earth and dismiss the monster by sitting your students down and asking them: "What do you want?" "What actions do you play?" "What is our Theme?" "What are we hoping to achieve with our story?" You will see shoulders relax and light bulbs go off— "Oh yeah's…" will fill the room.

- Acting well is expected. Poor acting is not.

- This performance is not about the students or the village, it is 100% about the audience.

- The actor's mantra before going on stage is: "Who am I? Where am I? What do I want?" This holds true whether you are doing the school play or Broadway—these three simple questions will send vital messages to the central nervous system bypassing the unnecessary brain chatter ("I hope they like me, what's my line, how do I look, am I good enough, blah-blah-blah?") with appropriate stage focus direction.

- Remind the village that the ultimate review of their work is not "That was an awesome play, you guys are great, great acting!" The ultimate review you are searching for is "Me too."

It is always an important concept to use acting, drama, and theater vocabulary when you are staging the story with your students. It might be a good idea to review the terminology and definitions I provided for you in **Prologue II**. Using this language will emphasize the high standard of performance you are expecting from the village. This language is industry standard and will assist in filtering out those ideas that might bring a less than serious intention to the work. Story building is hard work—use this language to emphasize your high expectations. If you were teaching Architecture, you would never allow your students to say "Could you pass me that metal thing over there." You would insist they used the term 'compass.' If you were teaching chemistry, you would never allow your students to say "You know, the smallest piece of a something." You would insist they used the term 'atom.' Story building might be fun, non-traditional, and collaborative, but it is also as serious and important as Architecture and Science (if not more).

We Before Me: Student Ownership of Story

Do you remember the Ubuntu story in in Act I: Building the Village? Those little African boys couldn't imagine one of their friends being sad while others were happy—the importance of the *We* far outweighed the importance of *Me*. As you can see throughout this book, this concept of *We before Me* is extremely important to me as a teacher and an essential core ingredient in the story building process. I have seen marvelously gifted actors perform poorly in horrendous productions because the director never attended to nurturing the community. In the west we have learned to place the individual's needs before the community's needs. It's the American Dream after all, right? In this dream our primary responsibility is to make sure we take as much fruit as possible and let the other slower folks fend for themselves—they all had the same opportunity, right? Accumulate as much stuff individually without concern for others and you will get more, bigger stuff until you have a mountain of stuff, also known as power. Only in America where the streets are paved in gold and money grows on trees! I am hopeful this is as shocking for you to read as it is sad for me to write but left on our own, we Westerners have been rewired to accumulate and colonize for personal gain. I say 're-wired' because this is not how we are designed or wired. There is a difference between what has become familiar and what is natural. We are naturally inclined to communicate, collaborate, and connect. Go observe a preschool playground to prove this point. You will not see the students running over each other to accumulate the most 'fruit.' You will see our beautiful natural design on full display: children communicating, collaborating, and connecting. I am not suggesting its one peace festival with multiple kumbaya moments. I am suggesting the idea of 'We before Me' will not be difficult to find. Fast forward several years to the highly competitive world of applying for colleges and observe this playground. Or skip a few more years ahead and observe the top business or graduate programs in the west. Taking turns to go down the slide has been replaced by the willingness to do just about anything to 'get ahead.'

I have some dear Burmese refugee friends who live near me in Buffalo. Several years ago, when these friends had just arrived in America, they were looking for a space to hold a large cultural event on our campus and asked for my help. I was happy to oblige and showed them one of our large theater spaces as a possible location. As we toured the space, my friends were speaking amongst each other in lengthy Burmese dialogues occasionally broken by the English phrase "American system" and then returning to Burmese. I observed this for several minutes until I asked, "I'm not sure what you are all saying but I do hear you say 'American system' every so often—what are you referring too?" My friend with the best English gently broke the news to me, "Professor Drew, as we think about our event, we want to make sure everyone who attends is free to eat as much as they'd like without having to pay money. We don't want them to think each person has to pay for themself to eat, but we don't have a word for that in Burmese because it never happens in our culture, so we say, 'American system'. No matter who you are or where you are from, if there is food available you can eat without question—its expected where we are from." I was both embarrassed and delighted—embarrassed by the shame of the American system and delighted to learn there was actually no word in Burmese for this! Despite the absurd and arrogant opinions of some of our nation's 'leaders', we have MUCH to learn from our New American brothers and sisters. I hope this conversation is opening our heart to the importance of these lessons you have the opportunity and responsibility to teach our young people. It may not surprise you to learn, that I believe the root of every major social, economic, and political issue plaguing our country today (political bipartisanship, violent crime, drugs, suicide, mass shootings, racism, religious intolerance, etc.) can be traced directly to replacing our natural inclination to communicate, collaborate and connect with our familiar inclination to silently strive for personal gain and disconnect from others.

So, do you need to take your students to Burma or Rwanda to learn (relearn) the power of We before Me? I would highly recommend it but realize the impracticality of such a demand. In the meantime, the story building process is an ideal vehicle to teach, illustrate and activate this lesson in multiple formats and arenas. At the story-sharing stage of the work, when your students are now ready to connect their work publicly, they must take full ownership of their story. As they prepare for performance (classroom, theater, auditorium, cafeteria, etc.) they must walk through the space together to decide what will happen where. There may be a large pillar where the mountain used to be—how will the village adapt? The students must make these choices. As the audience enters the space it is up to the students to gather backstage, out of audience view, and 'circle up' to prepare for the work of the village. It is the student's responsibility to warm up collectively and 'get right' for the performance using focus and group exercises. It is the student's responsibility to introduce the play to the audience. This short speech can provide helpful context for the story to be seen and the speaker should be rotated amongst the village. The post show talkback and workshop should be facilitated by the students as well. This moving from *student actor* to *student facilitator* is a crucial transition for the AFP story building work. I will share details of the post show talk back and interactive workshop in the next chapter.

So, what do you see missing in the ownership phase of the work? You are correct, *You* are missing! This is the ultimate teaching success—to no longer be needed. Truthfully and simply put, the entire story building process is a combination of steps and sequences whereby your students take the work from you so that it is theirs. You speak a lot in the beginning because you know more. From that point on, you should be speaking less and less while your students, the Village, speak more and more. Your teacher radar will highlight those ownership milestones throughout the process. When your students demand personal ownership, stop talking, just listen and imagine a picture of you, lips pursed with your index finger lightly touching them to suggest "Shhhh."

#Breadcrumb Alert#

A therapist friend of mine once shared a valuable lesson with me about choosing or not choosing to speak. The guide to this lesson was an acronym W.A.I.T., which stands for **Why Am I Talking?** *Am I talking to be heard? Am I talking to use the situation as a platform for an unrelated idea? Am I talking to make myself feel better, smarter or more confident? Am I talking because it is an honest contribution to the issue at hand? Am I talking because it would be best for my students? Am I talking because I don't trust what I have said before? Am I talking because I don't trust my students? Am I talking because it's necessary? There is also an obvious and powerful self-direction to pause embedded in WAIT. Stop, breathe and consider the authentic need for your voice. This is a healthy lesson to pass along to your students and (gulp) colleagues.*

You, of course, cannot leave and go on vacation once the ownership bell has sounded. Your presence at this phase is no less crucial than earlier, just much quieter. You must continue to provide feedback for your students regarding their story, the performance, and their consistent application of the village rules. You must be present to remind them of why they are sharing this story in the first place by as they their heads will drift to visions of Hollywood and Broadway; you must bring them back to the theme of their story. You must be present to remind them how important *We before Me* really is. Like every lesson woven through this process, it will be more effective the more the teacher highlights and values it. Don't be shy, you have a lot of rewiring to do—Ubuntu.

Poster for AFP student devised story LEVEL UP!
Students LOVE to see their work in print.
Legitimize Village ownership—Engage students to design the posters too!
100% Student Create = 100% Student owned

Poster for AFP student devised story TRASH
100% student created = 100% student owned

"Tell me and I forget.
Teach me and I remember.
Involve *me and I learn."*

Chinese Proverb

Act V: The Workshop
Activating the Lessons of the Story

There is nothing worse than being fully engaged in a meaningful story on stage, the lights come up, everyone stands up and goes home. This is the definition of heart-stopping disappointment! What is the audience to do with the multiple lessons they were just forced to ingest? When will they be able to digest all the thoughts, feelings, conflicts and questions? This is the western routine: The lights go out and we are transported to magical places where incredible things happen to extraordinary people under amazing circumstances. We have the opportunity to mirror our most important ideals, philosophies and struggles against those of the fictional world before us. We are the fortunate recipients of a moralistic call to action! The call is clear after the 'two hours traffic' on stage before us. The action...is...well...not quite as clear. In fact, we almost never have the opportunity to process the stories we see on stage. There is an arrogant assumption by us theater folk that the audiences have their lives to use as processing gyms once our work is done. You have been showered by our greatness, now go improve your lives, our work is done here, we will do it again tomorrow night! As you well know, the speed of our lives, the multiple distractions, and the swift turnaround of the 'news day' all make for convenient excuses to discard the authentic processing of the stories we see. Since most stories deal with harsh realities, it is certainly more comfortable not to personally process them. The human animal will avoid pain (or assumptive pain) at all costs. So, what are we if not walking time bombs waiting to emotionally explode at the slightest hint (almost always unexpected) of reference from a recently witnessed story? Should we simply stop watching stories to save ourselves from this struggle? Of course not—we couldn't reduce our enormous appetite for stories if we tried! (See Introductory Note: *Why Stories?)* The answer is not eliminating access to stories, the answer is adding experiential processing opportunities following the story's performances. The Anne Frank Project will never perform any of our student-devised performances without an interactive workshop immediately following the performance.

It is ironic that we must consistently remind the village that the story is not the most important product of the story building experience. I have mentioned several times throughout this book that the process of building stories is merely the vehicle that carries the important lessons of community building, conflict resolution and identity exploration. Allow me to reduce the importance of the story as product even further: The story performance is only there to open the door to the most important part of our school visits—the workshop. Apply the Chinese proverb above as your template for this important lesson:

"Tell me and I forget"

Teacher: "Work hard and good things happen!"

Student: (Information forgotten within moments—just talk).

"Teach Me and I Remember."

Teacher: "Work hard and good things happen. It will be on the test."

Student: (Information remembered for the test to ensure grade—forgotten soon afterward.)

"Involve me and I learn."

Teacher: "We are going to break into collaborative groups to create short stories to show what hard work looks like and what it provides."

Student: (the physical investment and personal responsibility has moved the concept of hard work from the brain to the heart via the body—lesson learned forever.)

"Involve me and learn" is really where AFP hangs its hat. We are so committed to this ideal that we ask out students never to finish the devised plays they are creating. This can be frustrating for them as they really want to tie the bow on the gift they have worked so hard to create. There is also the added satisfaction of knowing what happens to the protagonist(s) they have created and grown to care so much about. It can be quite unsatisfying to leave characters and situations 'hanging' in limbo. These concerns are typically calmed when I remind the village of our original intent: to teach the theme, the lesson of the play. My students know that experiencing is real learning, so they eventually accept this request to not finish the story—that's the audience's job. How will the students (in the audience) activate the lessons of the play? How can we leave the school with the confidence that the students in the audience will not just be *thinking* of the story's lessons, but they will have *practiced* the lessons of the play? Our central question that leads us into the creative process of every workshop: What would *you* do? The *you* is the student audience members of course.

The interactive workshop following the performances is one of my favorite moments of the process—every time. At the end of every AFP play, the students introduce themselves to the audience by their real names as they transition to the workshop. This accomplishes several objectives:

1. It breaks the fiction the play was presented in and returns to 'normal.'

2. It connects AFP students with the students in the audience on a personal level.

3. It transitions AFP students from 'actor' to 'facilitator.' My students facilitate the workshops. The high school students LOVE being attended to by superhero college students!

So, what do these workshops look like? How do you create them? What is the process? These are all great questions—questions you as teachers are uniquely prepared to answer because you do this all the time. Activating the lessons of the play is no different than devising an assessment for a required piece of literature or a class lesson unpacking a particular historical period. The central difference is that the workshop must involve the student audience kinesthetically. If you already use physical, experiential pedagogy in your classes, you are closer than you think. If you're a traditional teacher itching to break the chains of passive, cerebral learning, you just need a nudge and a long drink of courage.

Working with high school students for 90 minutes does not equate a full picture of each student, their history, or their story. The student's immediate 'opening up' to us can give the impression of us being closer than we actually are. This is why we mandate that school counselors (social workers, psychologists) are present for every performance/workshop AFP facilitates. There can also be an assumption that if a student is not fully participating in the workshop, then they are somehow being disrespectful of us or disinterested in what we are doing. This is, of course, untrue. We have no idea what happened to that particular student last week, yesterday last night or the class before our assembly. It is presumptuous for us to impose participation mandates on students who we just met. We have a saying in AFP about this: "If the student is in the room, they are participating." High school students are clever—if they wanted to be out of the room, they would find a way to get there (sudden filled bladder, headache, forgot a meeting with a teacher, etc.). My students have been trained to allow each student to have their personal experience. Physically committing to a feeling in front of others may simply be too much for a specific child to imagine, let alone do! Often, the quietest kids are the ones who are absorbing the most. We hear this from teachers and counselors time and time again. I share a personal story with my students often to illustrate this point. The first year we began touring we found ourselves in a typical local urban school filled with a diverse student body (predominantly African and Latin Americans), from low income, marginalized neighborhoods. There was a heavy-set boy sitting by himself, arms crossed, and a permanent angry scowl on his face throughout our performance/workshop. He had an empty seat on each side of him—the result of the fear his classmates felt for him. He watched every moment of the play intensely. He watched every moment of the workshop intensely—from his throne, not moving an inch. At the conclusion of the workshop the students were leaving the auditorium, returning to their classrooms and my students were packing up. As we made our way out of the auditorium towards the parking lot my shirt was tugged from behind—it was the heavy-set boy, "Hey mister, can I tell you something?" His eyes were welling up, "Thanks for coming to our school—nobody ever told me I mattered before you." I was without words. I grabbed his hand and brought him to me for a quick 'street' hug and said, "Well now you know—you do, you matter." He looked at me through those little-boy-trying-to-be-a-man eyes, said "uh-huh" and walked away. Point being: *If the student is in the room, they are participating.*

Rather than listing a step-by-step process for devising your accompanying workshop, I will share three workshops my students and I have created in recent years. A general step-by-step process will be difficult as each workshop takes on the spirit, structure, and flavor of the story it supports—every workshop is gloriously different!

Dear Me: **Story Summary**

Meet Reggie, a popular high school senior who is wrestling with the disturbing reality that his childhood pal, Charlie, has just committed suicide. Ignoring Reggie's desperate pleas, Charlie had recently *come out-of-the-closet* for all to know—the social impact was disastrous. After Charlie's funeral Reggie seeks the refuge of their childhood hideout in the woods—amidst symbols of their lifelong friendship Reggie writes a letter to Charlie hoping his unspoken thoughts will somehow reach his lost friend. Reggie's letter conjures much more than he plans for as souls from the past magically visit him to aid his journey towards self-discovery, emotional maturity and inner peace.

The Process:

Dear Me is the product of a theater collaboration initiated in Rwanda, January 2013. A group of SUNY Buffalo State students, faculty and alumni traveled to east Africa as part of The Anne Frank Project's global programming. The Buffalo State team collaborated with Rwandan students, artists, and teachers to create the foundation for their own, original play. The letter-writing element reflects a current national focus in Rwanda—a commitment to the "next step" of post genocide education where survivors celebrate their lost loved ones through thousands of letters creating a "Book of Life." This marks a significant moment in Rwanda's emotional, intellectual, and national recovery. The American team was deeply touched by this process and decided to devote their spring 2013 semester to developing this powerful idea into a play that they, The Anne Frank Project, would share with local schools. While the genesis is purely Rwandan, the product is a universal story tailored for today's American high school students. Issues of belonging, friendship, self-identity, bullying, bystanders, and conflict resolution are explored through the eyes of multiple global cultures. Buffalo State student artists perform the play and lead the hands-on workshop immediately following each performance. We hope to leave each school having provided tools and vocabulary for positive community building thus reinforcing the central message of *Dear Me*: **You can always connect.**

Theme: *You Can Always Connect*

Performance: 30 minutes

Workshop: 30-60 minutes

*Must fit performance and workshop within traditional school periods (35-40 minutes)

Immediately following the performance there will be a brief Q&A. While many topics can be covered ("How long did it take you to write that play?"), the discussion should always end on theme: *What was the theme, message or lesson of the story you just watched?* (5 minutes).

Before all workshops we share the following AFP mandate:

"You matter. Your story matters. We are here to help you tell your story, because if you don't tell your story someone else will and they're going to get it wrong"

Workshop:

1. Prompt-paper/pen distributed to each audience member:

    "The theme of the play you just saw is 'You can always connect.' Reggie felt better after he reached out to Charlie through his letter. Take a moment and write a letter to someone or something you feel the need to connect with. There is no right or wrong, these won't be graded and only those who wish to share will share."

2. Find someone to share your letter with out loud. Listen with respect and care. Share your responses to each other's letters. What *adjective* best describes each other's letters?

3. Exchange letters and read them aloud as if they were *your own* stories. Handle each other's stories with care and no judgment. *What if this were you?*

   - Brief explanation of the power of theater and imagination. Emphasize the difference between literal and figurative, realistic and. abstract. Encourage imagination, theatricality, and creativity. Discourage being 'real.'

4. Story-Build #1

   Who is the exact person, place or thing (voice) of your letter?*Who* is speaking? Share your letters with each other emphasizing the *Who*.

5. Story-Build #2

   Who is the exact person, place or thing (target) your letter is speaking to? *Who* is it for? Share your letters with each other emphasizing the *Who(s)*.

6. Story-Build #3

   Where (environment) does your letter take place? What's the best possible location? Encourage abstract thinking (i.e. a cloud made of cotton candy) vs. literal thinking (i.e. a room in school). Share your letters with each other emphasizing the *Where*—emphasize **physical** communication.

7. Story-Build #4

   Collaborate with your partner to decide which of the two letters you'd like to choose for the next step, bringing your letter to life. Which letter has the most immediate *physical* reaction? Which would be best to see on stage? Decipher which would be the best for this process not the favorite, most popular, etc. *Story* first, trust your gut.

8. Story-Build #5

   Share the story with each other exaggerating the physicality. Allow the physical to evolve from *real* to *abstract*. As a team, select **three adjectives** that best describe the feelings of the letter/story. Repeat physical sharing until adjectives are surfaced and agreed upon.

9. Who would like to share their *Who, Who, Where* and *Adjectives* with everyone?

10. Story-Build #6

    * Who would like to share their letter/story with everyone?

    * Announce your Who, Who, Where and Adjectives

    * Share your letter with everyone out loud

    * Request volunteers to be *physical-adjectives*

    * Rehearse physical-adjectives

    * Repeat letter/story sharing supported by physical-adjectives

    * **Repeat #10 until allotted time is finished.**

When Ana is pulled through her bedroom mirror she faces
fantastical worlds filled with moments of reflection and
discovery. She meets bizarre characters and defeats her
biggest insecurities to start learning to love her story.

Mirror/rorriM: Story Summary

When Anna is pulled through her bedroom mirror, she faces fantastical worlds filled with moments of reflection and discovery. She
meets bizarre characters and defeats her biggest insecurities to
start learning to love her story. Anna's 'other self' is the one who
pulls her through the mirror and into her journey of self-discovery.
This reflection of herself is played by a male named Rex—Rex,
like all other characters Anna meets in mirror-land, only speaks
in poetic rhymes. This elevated text helps to define the lessons
learned, the heightened stakes of the journey and the magic of
the environment.

The Process:

This story was built by students whose collective response to their Rwanda trip was one of awe, inspiration, and acceptance. The students were particularly impressed by the Rwandans they met who were passionately and lovingly loving their story. What was a population filled with grief and loss had become a population rallying around their present story? They refused to be identified by the 1994 Genocide. While this was certainly part of the Rwandan story it was not the entirety of the Rwandan story. The students met contemporary Rwandans who embraced their pre-colonial history filled with beautiful customs, rituals and ceremonies. The students met contemporary Rwandans whose pride of present-day Rwanda was palpable at every turn. My students beamed with vicarious pride at the amazing Rwanda recovery and reconciliation process; Rwanda had clearly learned to love their story.

Theme: *Learn to Love Your Story*

Performance: 30 minutes

Workshop: 30-60 minutes

Must fit performance and workshop within traditional school periods (35-40 minutes)

Immediately following the performance there will be a brief Q&A. While many topics can be covered ("How long did it take you to write that play?"), the discussion should always end on theme: *What was the theme, message, or lesson of the story you just watched?* (5 minutes).

Before all workshops we share the following AFP mandate:

You matter.

Your story matters.

The only way things move forward is when people share their stories. Negative things happen when people don't share their stories. Silence is a dirty word. When you have a story to tell, and you choose silence you are a **Bystander**.

Workshop:

1. Prompt: The actor who played Rex shares the epilogue of the play (again). This is Rex's final lesson to Anna and the audience:

   Though Ana is stronger than when we first met Her journey's not over, we cannot forget. As we turn the page, we see she's not alone: We all have problems that are not always shown. As we close this book, open yours and look in What battles inside are you fighting to win? Your lions and demons and beasts from below You'll never be free if you can't let them go. Turn the page and you'll see you have stories to tell Your journey starts now, so good luck, and farewell.

2. What was unique about what you just heard? What is poetry? Rhyme? Metered language? Why do we use poetry? Why does Rex speak in rhyme in mirror-land?

3. Just using the sounds (Ba-Ba...) let's hear the meter music of Rex's epilogue.

4. Meter is like rap. Does meter make you want to move? Let's do the Ba-Ba exercise again, but this time with movement. Let your body do what it wants to do with the "music" of the meter.

5. Story-Build #1

   The theme of *Mirror/rorriM* is "Learn to Love Your Story." Can you imagine writing a meter-rap expressing your love of YOUR story? Write down/think of three adjectives that describe YOUR story.

6. Story-Build #2

   Find a partner. Share your three adjectives with your partner. After you have shared them verbally, activate them by sharing them physically. Share your adjectives verbally and physically with each other. How do they make you feel?

7. Story-Build #3

   Switch adjectives with your partner—verbally/physically express each other's adjectives. How were they similar and/or different from your own?

8. Story-Build #4

   Remember the meter-music Rex used (Ba-Ba...). Working with your partner, create the first four lines of YOUR story using the meter-music structure. Share your story rhymes with each other.

9. Story-Build #5

   Add your bodies to your story rhymes as you share them. Allow your voices to work together with our bodies to fully share YOUR stories.

10. Story-Build #6

   Find another group of story partners and combine to make your group 4 or more. Teach your story rhymes to each other, one at a time. As you teach yours, the other three must verbally and physically activate them, own them, respect them with commitment. It should be a loud room filled with you "Learning to Love Your Stories."

11. Story-Build #7

   Who would like to share their rhyme story with everyone on stage? You can share it individually or in your groups. The rule: You must use your voices and your bodies when sharing YOUR stories.

Hello, My Name Is _____: Story Summary

Meet Alex, a young girl who lives in a future world where individual identity is forbidden, and conformity mandated. A moment of inspiration launches her into a journey through mystical lands and dangerous obstacles. Will Alex brave the unknown to claim her identity or will she surrender to the status quo? Alex learns she must embrace her struggles in order to celebrate herself. Interactive workshop immediately follows performance focusing on identity exploration, peer pressure and social conformity.

The Process:

Theme: *You Must Embrace Your Struggles to be Yourself*

Performance: 30 minutes

Workshop: 30-60 minutes

Must fit performance and workshop within traditional school periods (35-40 minutes)

Immediately following the performance there will be a brief Q&A. While many topics can be covered ("How long did it take you to write that play?"), the discussion should always end on theme: *What was the theme, message, or lesson of the story you just watched?* (5 minutes).

Before all workshops we share the following AFP mandate:

"You matter.

Your story matters.

The only way things move forward is when people share their stories. Negative things happen when people don't share their stories. Silence is a dirty word. When you have a story to tell and you choose silence you are a **Bystander.**"

Workshop:

1. Prompt: How many of you (students) have good thoughts about yourselves? How many of you have bad thoughts about yourself? That makes you like 100% of the people we've ever met! Having a variety of thoughts is completely normal—in fact, it's your bran's job to keep having thoughts. But…not every thought your brain creates is

true. Your brain is just trying to protect you with as many thoughts as possible. YOU are in control of which thoughts you like and which thoughts you don't—which thoughts are good and which thoughts are bad. Not all your thoughts are automatically equal—not all your thoughts accurately describe you.

2. Do you remember when Alex was stuck in the bottom of the hole? How did she feel? How would you feel? What thoughts were going through Alex's head? What thoughts would go through your head? How were Alex's good thoughts symbolized in the play (Bubbles)? What did those bubbles do for Alex? Yes, they elevated her out of the hole to safety so she could continue her journey. Your good thoughts can help elevate you out of your dark places too. Let's do an exercise to help you separate your GOOD thoughts from your BAD thoughts.

3. Mindfulness 1:

   Put your feet flat on the floor, hands on your knees, close your eyes and imagine a helium balloon gently lifting the top of your heard and spine. Let's take three breaths together: Inhaling slowly through the nose, exhaling slowly through the mouth. We exhale through our mouths because breaths are thoughts and thoughts are combined to create stories—we want your body to know you are preparing to share your story—can't do that through your nose

4. Mindfulness 2:

   After we have taken three breaths together, as a story-building village, continue to take your slow, clam breaths at your own speed. You will notice your brain wanting to be involved creating lots of thoughts—for now, just answer each thought with directing all your attention to the present moment—no thinking about the past or future, just redirect yourselves to the NOW. Only pay attention to what's happening in the present moment. Simple Direction: *Be With What Is.*

5. Mindfulness 3:

   While you are breathing calmly, with your body in a place of relaxed dignity, continue your focus on the NOW while you follow this image: Imagine your brain, your thought factory, to be a large tree with many branches. Now imagine your thoughts as birds that come and land on these branches—some invited, some not. Some of these birds are negative and scary: these are birds bringing bad thoughts to your tree (*You're not good enough, You're ugly, etc.*) Some of these birds are positive and happy: these birds are bringing good thoughts to your tree (*You're a great person, People like you, etc.*)

6. Mindfulness 4:

   This is YOUR tree, so you're in charge of which birds can stay and which will be asked to leave. Here's the trick: before inviting or dismissing birds, you MUST acknowledge that they do indeed exist in the NOW. SEE the bird/thought, ACKNOWLEDGE the bird/thought, KEEP/DISPOSE the bird/thought.

7. Story-Build #3

   Switch adjectives with your partner—verbally/physically express each other's adjectives. How were they similar and/or different from your own?

8. Story-Build #4

   Remember the meter-music Rex used (Ba-Ba...). Working with your partner, create the first four lines of YOUR story using the meter-music structure. Share your story rhymes with each other.

9. Story-Build #5

   Add your bodies to your story rhymes as you share them. Allow your voices to work together with our bodies to fully share YOUR stories.

10. Story-Build #6

    Find another group of story partners and combine to make your group 4 or more. Teach your story rhymes to each other, one at a time. As you teach yours, the other three must verbally and physically activate them, own them, respect them with commitment. It should be a loud room filled with you "Learning to Love Your Stories."

11. Story-Build #7

    Who would like to share their rhyme story with everyone on stage? You can share it individually or in your groups. The rule: You must use your voices and your bodies when sharing YOUR stories.

"Knowledge is power.
Information is liberating.
Education is the premise of progress,
in every society, in every family."

Kofi Annnan

Epilogue:
Testimonials and Connections

This section shares the many testimonials and real-world applications of story-based learning from our partners around the globe. Featuring K-12 classrooms, higher-education studios and community organizations, these shared stories will 'walk the bridge' from theory to application in variety of settings and disciplines.

Our most sincere hope is that your unique SBL experiences can be added to this chapter to share with others —just email them to me: kahanj@buffalostate.edu. The village will continue to grow as we bring SBL into the hearts and minds of young people around the world and you will have the opportunity to collaborate with and learn from other story-builders.

This section is intentionally fluid and constantly being updated by new partners and collaborators. Please scan the code below to review the most current contributors to the global library of testimonials and applications of AFP's SBL!

Finale: Resources

Books, Research, Scholarship, Websites

The world of arts-based education systems, approaches and platforms continues to grow and expand. The community of practitioners and facilitators also expands regularly: we are educators, professors, artists, businesswomen/men, researchers, and parents. The research stretches to accommodate this amazing community and its diverse set of practices, coming from a variety of sources, disciplines, and value systems. In a word, this explosion of scholarship is **Thrilling!** To capture this excitement, I share with you the AFP bibliography—always growing, always developing, always sharing new ideas so that we can bring the very best to our students, their stories, and their learning processes. Please scan the code below to access AFP's most recent combination of resources for SBL.

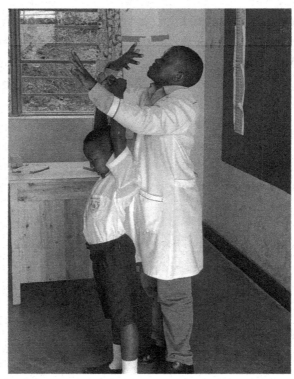

"We agree we cannot do it alone."

AFP Village Rule

Acknowledgements

Due to the communal nature of this work, it should be clear by now that my work represents the accumulation of countless 'villages', countless 'villagers' and countless stories. If I were to list all of those who have contributed to my research, this book would be thousands of pages. This list grows every week as does my understanding, appreciation, and respect for the story building process. I am honored to witness the stories shared by so many for the past 30 years and counting. I am humbled by the trust invested, the courage mustered, and the discipline applied. I have the greatest job in the world—I am inspired every day.

To my family:

Thank you to my heart, my best friend and dear wife Maria. There is no one whose hand I grasp tighter, whose soul I admire greater, whose smile I crave more than yours—Namaste'. Thank you to my amazing children—Sam, your soaring, fierce creativity informs every chapter of my story. Nate, your fiery soul, unimaginable patience, and explosive heart forge my path forward—you are the definition of *Toughness* and *Grace*. To my mother whose lessons echo throughout this book, my classrooms and life. There is no Professor Kahn without you—period. To 'Zadie,' my dad who brought generosity, stability, and unconditional love to a family when we needed it most. To my brother and sister who provided protection for their 'little Drew' so his story could be realized. To my

Baubie—you are with me every day to remind me that everyone's story matters regardless of their place in life. To my Zadie who taught me that suffering cannot stop our stories, it just requires more work—and work is good.

To my students:

You are the foundation for all I have done professionally, all I do and all I continue to learn. Your trust and faith in me have given me more fuel and pride than you will ever know. You are the fire that constantly warms my story—thank you for the countless lessons I have learned from you and for those to come. When I think of my research, I think of you. Quite literally you ARE my book. Thank you for allowing me to share you in so many ways. You are SO much more interesting than this book—thank you for understanding that.

To my teachers and schools:

From Buffalo to Los Angeles and every U.S. stop in between. From Rwanda to Kenya, Switzerland to the Netherlands, Burma to Japan—thank you for sharing your culture's stories. To all the schools, systems, governments, and organizations that have dared to make story building part of their institutions. To all the outstanding teachers, educators, and administrators I have had the immense privilege to work with. Thank you for embracing the fact that you and your students matter. Thank you for teaching me, sharing with me, and exploring with me. You are amazing individuals doing amazing things for your students. We are forever bound by common story—AFP is better because of your membership in the 'Village.' I realize weaving story building through the fabric of contemporary education is not easy. You are the embodiment of one of my favorite quotes by Wayne Dyer: "In order to walk on higher ground you must be willing to be separate from the popular opinion of others." Thank you for your courage.

To the leadership of SUNY Buffalo State:

Thank you for your unflinching support of the Anne Frank Project and the work of story-based learning. My research is not traditional—you have always realized its value despite the loud noise of academia's fear of change. I have always felt great freedom to do the right thing. Buffalo State is a unique and important place to work—that is largely due to the inspired leadership of the past (Dr. Muriel Howard, Dr. Dennis Ponton, Dr. Melanie Perreault) and particularly our current President, Dr. Katherine Conway-Turner, Provost James Mayrose and Associate Provost Amitra Wall. It is a pleasure to serve the State University of New York with you. Onward.

To my special teachers:

Thank you to the countless genocide survivors who have shared your stories, your families, your smiles, your generous spirits, and delicious food with me. Your courage astounds me. Your smiles amaze me. Your lessons inspire me. In particular, my second family, remarkable Rwanda—you deserve every bright story that comes your way. Your ability to rewrite your national narrative following 1994 has completely reconfigured my idea of what human beings are capable of. I am fortunate to be made of the same stuff as you. *Murakoze cyane, Urukundo Na Amahoro.*

To my best Dutch girlfriend Sophia Veffer. Thank you for bringing the light of Anne Frank to so many, the perspective of unfiltered honesty to so many and, most importantly, the person of Sophia Veffer to so many. We are a better world because of you Sophia. I am a better person because of you Sophia. There is no AFP without you Sophia. I know you will hate to read these accolades of you—too bad, you matter too much. *Tikun Olam.*

To Anne Frank and all the 'Anne Franks' fighting for clarity, decency and freedom despite the enormous obstacles the world has put before you. It is your stories we strive to tell with the bravery, grace and hope you teach us every day.